THE 17TH SUITCASE

THE 17TH SUITCASE

Rev. Samuel Moonsamy & Family

Paperback Edition October 2, 2020
ISBN 978-0-578-41989-3

Dedicated to our grandchildren
Alec, Kaitlyn, Alisha, Karissa, Daniel,
and the generations to come

FOREWORD

If the humorous or sad experiences referenced in these vignettes mirror some of your experience, we encourage you to tell your story too. The generations to come have so much to learn, but they will not know, unless we tell. If you have overcome a hurt, an indignity and you are still surviving, or you are thriving, then you may relate to some of the stories on the pages that follow.

We finally heeded the call to select some of our parents' stories to share, between full time jobs, some of us while raising families. We did so, because whenever they speak to groups, no matter how small or large, they are inevitably asked, "Have you written a book?" Even with small blurbs or funny anecdotes that dad shares on social media, someone responds that he should share these thoughts and experiences in a book. If you have ever posed this sort of question or comment, we thank you for this measure of encouragement. It means more than you will ever know.

As we read through the pieces that dad had written over a span of 60 years, we had to stop often, to allow the power of each story to sink in. It inspired some of us to add our own experiences. Our profound respect for our parents grew stronger (and still does) with each reminder of all that they had to endure and overcome, often for us, their children, so that we could have a better life than they could only dream of, for themselves.

Dad started writing short stories in his early twenties, on a second-hand typewriter. It is clear that he has a literary bent, a knack for speaking and writing. In South Africa, we recall how he would make letters sound official when parishioners would come to him for help with legal documentation for a court or an administrative office. More of a teacher than a "fire and brimstone" preacher, dad weaves funny or thought-provoking stories into his sermons, making them come alive. He has published articles in newspapers and journals in South Africa and in the United States. An avid reader, in addition to the many books he reads, he reads the bible and the entire newspaper everyday.

Dad started churches in Lenasia, Merebank, Chatsworth and Pietermaritzburg and pastored two more at Newclare and Noordgesig, in South Africa. In the United States, dad started a little church in Richmond, California which he continued to run in Pinole, California, on a monthly basis. We cannot even begin to count the additional churches and community events where he has taken us to minister over the years, and still does at 83 years young! If we have had the opportunity to share with you at some point in this way, we thank you. We can assure you that it has been a tremendous blessing to us. Likewise, dad says that he has gained more from his mentorship of many young pastors and leaders, than they could ever have gained from him. God has used him and mom to touch so many lives, particularly the lives of their six children, their four children's spouses, and their five grandchildren!

We love you and salute you for your strength and perseverance, mom and dad, and for raising us to love God and to seek Him in all that we do!

The Moonsamy "Children"
Priscilla, Susheela, Ursula, Melanie, Neil and Noelene

Contents

1

JOHANNESBURG COUNTRY CLUB

by Samuel Moonsamy

KNOWN throughout the world as the premier venue where the rich and the famous play, sing, wine, dine, and dance in high fashion, I remember the Johannesburg Country Club because my father worked there as a waiter, for 40 years of dedicated service.

He retired in the late 1950's, without a handshake or a penny for retirement, only the memory of feeding and pampering the wealthy class of white South Africans, for a pittance as his pay. He earned his last month's salary and took home with him an amount of 12 pounds, the equivalent of about $25 at that time, sufficient to provide for his family for just a couple of weeks. He left with heart-wrenching sorrow for a future with nothing but a sick body to care for, and a large family, on whom he now depended, since he could no longer provide for them. Daily he had to carry an identity document with the word "Stateless/Staatloos" boldly emblazoned across the top which meant he did not belong in South Africa, the country of his birth, or anywhere in the world. This also indicated that he would never be allowed to acquire a passport for travel.

It was at this country club where my father with more or less 12 other Indian waiters, served faithfully day after day. The large impressive facility was situated on a manicured property, with lush green gardens, an 18 hole golf course, a swimming pool, and fancy dining rooms. The well-equipped kitchen, unequaled in splendor, gave forth the aroma of the best cooked meals every day of the year. Weekends were especially busy with functions such as golf tournaments, extravagant birthday parties, and stylish and sophisticated weddings.

After a day's work, the waiters who were going off shift, retired to the waiters' quarters near the back gate, guarded by a security guard who was a black man with a knob kierrie (a heavy stick with a knob at the end). No one dared challenge his authority.

My father worked every day and came home every other weekend. Whenever he arrived home, he brought with him a dozen baked goods, bananas, and some of the excess food. The food items that would usually be thrown out the following day at the country club, were considered a luxury to us. He also picked up chestnuts that fell from the trees, along the way home, which we boiled and ate. They were delicious, and helped fill his nine kids growling tummies.

After my dad retired, my brother and I worked some weekends as "extras," casual workers, normally from 5 pm to 1 am. Like chess pieces, all of the waiters, dressed in white coats

Brothers: Tommy (Boykie), Bobby and Sammy

with black pants, black ties, and white turbans, would stand at attention alongside the tables assigned to us for the night. Before our first night of work, my father had instructed me and my brother to stand up straight if a white person spoke to us.

The menus were displayed neatly in the center of the tables with white table cloths, knives, forks, spoons, fish knives and butter knives placed in precise order, with a place in the center for the plate. The prix fixe menu boasted twelve to twenty items starting with cocktail shrimp, sliced or diced melon, usually two to three kinds of soup, fish either fried, poached or steamed and several entrees supported by fresh sautéed vegetables. We served what was known as "silver service." This meant that the food was placed on extremely hot trays. We served the food from the hot tray to the plate, at the choice or request of the guest. Occasionally we became nervous and spilled food on the expensive clothing of chagrined and angry guests, who insulted us and also complained to the management.

On one occasion, a patron's dinner roll was not soft enough. Highly dissatisfied and angry, she pulled my older brother Tommy, whom we called Boykie, by the ear and told him what kind of bread roll he should bring to her table. With polite sarcasm, he swore at her in Tamil, an Indian language. When she asked what he was saying, he responded that he was saying "Sorry ma'am. I will get you another roll." He returned from the kitchen with the same bread roll, after he and a few of his waiter friends had played soccer with it on the floor, lightly tramping on it to soften it. He then dusted it off, and served it to her on a spotlessly clean new doily. She was satisfied now that the roll was much softer, and warned him to be careful next time and be sure to only bring such rolls, to her table.

Before the night was over my brother and some of his friends were completely drunk from all the alcohol they had stolen from the tables. To avoid being caught, they would empty the contents that were leftover from liquor bottles into empty coffee pots and carry them to the kitchen. At this time, Black South Africans were not allowed to buy or consume alcohol but Indians could purchase alcohol with a permit known as TARC (Transvaal Asiatic Registration Certificate).

At 12 am sharp, the largely English clientele would stand, as the band played "God Save the Queen." The esteemed guests would sit down again to be served bacon, eggs and sausages with thinly sliced melba toast and coffee.

We cleared the tables after all of the guests had left and headed for the kitchen to stand in line for our wages of 2 pounds, 2 shillings and 6 pence (approximately $4.50 in 1950), enough to provide about 2 meals for our family.

After 1:00am, in the early hours of the morning, we would

walk the two or three miles to Braamfontein station and wait for the 3 am train to Kliptown station. From there, we would walk another 3 or 4 miles to our home, arriving at the break of dawn, to sleep until late Sunday morning, before getting up for church.

Sometimes the stories my dad told came back to me. The time when they lived in Vrededorp about 4 or 5 miles from the Country Club where he worked in Auckland Park. After work, late at night, the waiters would board the last tram home. Young white people who had gone out to the movies and bars were usually returning home to Newlands or Vrededorp on the same tram. So-called Indians and Coloureds were allowed upstairs only, and they had to sit in the back circle which normally seated about 8 people. It became problematic, however, when passengers of color would try to step off the tram at their destinations. Young white hooligans would follow closely behind them from the top of the steel staircase or somewhere in between, and kick the Indian waiters who were getting off; sometimes they fell on top of each other like dominoes. On several occasions, they did this before the tram would come to a complete stop, watching and laughing hysterically as some of the waiters would fall to the bottom platform near the door. On one occasion, my dad's friend was kicked from the tram and was seriously injured. He never recovered from his injuries and died soon after. After this experience, my dad decided to walk the 4 miles from the Club to his home in Vrededorp. He never rode the tram again.

Waiters had a lingua franca of their own and often spoke about the white man and all the problems they had to undergo. Some of the stories were funny and some were sad. They told about what they would do to the people they served, who showed arrogance, and treated them sorely and with disrespect. Some of the stories were not so nice and some unmentionable. To this day I always maintain a cordial and friendly relationship with servers at restaurants or hotels. Firstly, they deserve that respect, and secondly, you never know what might happen behind closed kitchen doors.

Identification card of Cula Helepa Moonsamy (my father, fondly known as Papa). Despite being born in South Africa in the late 1800's, he was declared "stateless," having no country, thus not permitted to travel

2

HOW I SAVED A WHITE MAN FROM BEING BLACK

by Samuel Moonsamy

ALL of us in South Africa were either victims or victors of Apartheid, a systematized hierarchical humanization or dehumanization of people on the basis of color. Rarely was a white person "demoted" to a black person, when he was, de facto white. At a public facility, the Brixton Tower, ostensibly situated on a hill in Brixton about ten miles from the center of Johannesburg, I performed my "act of kindness."

It happened in the early seventies, when racial segregation was completely established and in place by almost all of the agencies of government: national, provincial, and local. To my knowledge, the Brixton Tower, also known as the Hertzog Tower and later the Sentech Tower, served as a transmission tower for the South African Broadcasting Corporation (SABC), and amongst other functions, housed a post office. The top of the tower offered a stunning view of the entire city of Johannesburg.

A man walked up to the reception area of the tower, to ask for admission to the observation deck on the top floor, for him and his family who were still outside in the car. Presumably, due to his obviously darker skin tone, he was told by the man behind the counter: "Sorry, you cannot go up today. Your people can only go up on Thursdays."

"Okay" the patron said and walked out slowly, looking confused.

Jy's 'n Blanke Persoon (You're a White Man)

Realizing the error, I followed the man outside and told him that the receptionist had mistaken him for "non-white." The handsome young man with his copper skin tone, probably the result of a suntan from a recent vacation to one of South Africa's "white" sandy beaches, returned with me. I led him up to the counter and explained that he was actually white and that he had the right to go up on any day. Without apology but visibly shaken and embarrassed, the official collected the amount due.

By this time the man's wife and daughter, obviously white and not sun tanned, had joined him inside, completely oblivious to the serious crack in Apartheid that had just occurred. The agent of Apartheid ascribed the wrong diagnosis causing a major human "error" which I, more so a sorry victim, corrected. The result was that the white man was granted permission to

8

go up but I was left sitting "low and dry."

The man who had just bought tickets for the observation deck, thanked me and smiled, shyly beckoning his family to the elevator. At that moment conflicting thoughts crossed my mind. I tried one more time to request to go up. The receptionist responded, "Absolutely not! "Nee, glad nie!" he replied in both English and Afrikaans.

Earlier, we had entered the lobby with my cousin Nain and his family who were visiting from Durban, a beautiful tropical city on the east coast of South Africa. We were excited to host our dear family and show them sights of our city, but were told to come back on Thursday, "Nanny's Day off." I should have known not to come by on this day from our Indian Township of Lenasia, 20 miles away, but I tried anyhow, hoping to find some grace and compassion.

I retreated to where my family was sitting. Looking at me and having seen the whole drama unfold, they began to laugh. I joined them in laughter, though we should have been crying, and then we walked around demurely looking at the pictures on the wall near the counter in the circular building. Disappointed, we returned home, with no desire to return again. Sadly, my children never had the opportunity to ascend the heights of this tower and enjoy the magnificent views from this iconic structure in Johannesburg. We never went back again.

The imposing, approximately 250 meter (800 foot) tall, Brixton Tower, situated in a declared white area overlooked a cemetery that was also white, except for an Indian crematorium nearby where people of Indian descent but native to South Africa, were allowed to cremate their dead. The air in this white area, polluted daily with Indian smoke going up through its tall chimneys was breathed by black and white alike. Why nobody complained about the Indian crematorium, no one knows. Maybe at a later time with the complete removal of the "black spots (term for black areas surrounded by white areas)," a new, more "suitably" situated crematorium, would be built in an area for "non whites."

Why Thursday? Here I am, a South African of Indian descent, saving a white man from being declared black or brown and restricted from going up this tower on a day other than a Thursday. On Thursdays, "Nanny's Day Off," most public amenities were open to people of color. During the other days of the week, but especially on the weekends, the "miesies'" (ma'am) and baas (boss) were either going out to the movies, or drinking and dancing at the clubs. The helpers (nannies or maids), usually black, were to remain with the kids, watching, cleaning, feeding, bathing and taking care of them, sometimes until the weekend was over and the "miesies" and "baas" returned home.

Because Thursday was the day of rest for the nanny, it also became a convenient excuse for the local Johannesburg government to use this day to make more money. On Thursdays, "non-whites" were allowed entry to public facilities, though strictly segregated at all times. Even on Thursdays, there were separate and very limited facilities, such as restrooms, for people of color. Then, the zoo was one of the facilities where blacks could go any day, though through a separate entrance and exit, with separate play facilities, drinking faucets, and toilets.

The incident at the tower brought back vivid memories of our visit to the Botanical Gardens in Durban, with our toddler, Priscilla and newborn, Susheela. We strolled along admiring the milkwoods, the purple splendor of the jacaranda, the sturdy national flower, the protea, and so many other blooms and blossoms, bathed in the warm African sunlight. With baby

Susheela in our arms, Priscilla did what most toddlers would do; she excitedly ran ahead and clambered onto a bench along the pathway. She turned to wave at us, a huge smile playing across her face. We waved back at her. Suddenly, a policeman seemed to appear from nowhere. He bolted toward our two-year old, brandishing a long stick. Sue and I ran toward her and she quickly jumped into the safety of my arms. She started to cry quietly as the policeman sternly warned us that the seating areas were reserved for "whites only."

Johannesburg, The Big City

My mind reverted back to the tower. From the top of the Brixton Tower, one could view the entire golden city. Another popular spot, the Carlton Center, is the tallest building in Johannesburg, standing at fifty stories high. People of color also frequented the Zoo Lake, a lake across from, as the name suggests, the zoo, particularly during the holidays, when decorative lights glistened on the water. Other than these select areas for outings and recreation, the drab and monotonous townships offered little to amuse and entertain kids and visitors of color who came to see the big city. In the Cape and Natal, people could visit the beaches, though these sandy beaches were also separated along color lines, limited by strict racial segregation laws. No one seemed to notice that the ocean waters mixed as the waves swept back and forth.

Just like the tower of Babel in the Bible, the immemorial Brixton Tower was built as a very visible point of pride and unity for those in control at the time. It still stands erect as an outstanding beacon proudly enhancing the tourist pictures showing the city as a vibrant modern world class city. Not many people know about the pain and humiliation it caused to promote the "civilized city" at the southern end of the continent by the people who considered themselves special and refused to disperse into the world.

The vision of the grand design of separation of the races has now been born again into a diversity of peoples and languages. Apartheid, like an unfinished building, stands out like a shameful sore thumb. To us the tower stands as a stark reminder of the past, a miserable memorial of an icon that died less than twenty years after we were turned away. Rising into the sky, the Brixton tower stands as a symbol, to us and the generations to come, of how far we have come and how much further we can push forward with hope, as the possibilities for the future are limitless.

3

A Day in Durban

by Samuel Moonsamy

O N April 19th 1962, less than three months after we were married, the Thursday before the long Easter weekend, my young wife Sue, just two weeks shy of her 17th birthday, and I, found ourselves at the bustling Park Station in Johannesburg. The Church had commissioned us 400 miles away, to start a new church in the largely Indian coastal city of Durban. We stood on the platform nervously, ready to embark on our journey.

By South African law which applied to Indians and Chinese, we were not allowed to cross over any provincial borders of the four provinces/states at the time, without a visitor's permit usually granted for three to six weeks for a nonrefundable fee of R10. Violators of this law would be penalized with a fine or imprisonment for a specified period of time.

A further restriction was that all permission for travel through the Orange Free State (OFS) was "in transit only." Indians were not allowed to stay overnight in this state and we understood that, if we were traveling by car and had to break down anywhere in this Province, we would have to report to the nearest police station. Ironically, this state was known as the "free" state. We joked about the system so as not to get too depressed. South Africans have an amazing sense of humor; laughter was medicine to our souls. One of the many jokes that we heard was:

"What is the fastest thing in South Africa?"

Answer: "An Indian on a bicycle riding through the Orange Free State."

We were issued a special permit for six weeks to be extended at the discretion of the authorities. With this document safely tucked away, we were ready to embark on our journey into the unknown.

Our train was to travel through the Transvaal lowveld for about 200 miles before crossing the border at Volksrust and on into Natal via Newcastle, through the winding Majuba Hills. It would arrive at Pietermaritzburg the next day, about fifty miles from our final destination. This particular train was known as the "fast train" or "express" that travelled overnight with dining facilities for whites only. Sleeping facilities were provided in the 2nd class non-white coach, but the 3rd class had no such provisions. Anyone with a ticket could squeeze into any 3rd class compartment, making the space very crammed and unsafe.

Our farewell party included my mother and five sisters Dolly, Villie, Rosie, Neela, and Thilla along with Sue's mum, and her brother Anand. After a prayer by mentor and friend Pastor Taylor, everyone tearfully sang "God be with you till we

Sam's mom and 7 of her children; Top row from left to right: Dolly, Huma, Sammy, Violet; Bottom row from left to right: Rosie, Kista, Neela, Villie; (Not included are Boykie, Bobby and Thilla and my dad's children from his deceased first wife: Doorsamy and Pakari)

meet again" (a song usually sung at funerals). During those days, a trip to Durban, just 400 miles away, was like a trip across the oceans. Our families did not know when they would ever see us again. They cried and we cried as the train slowly departed. This was Sue's first trip to Durban. She was afraid and sad to leave her family, so I tried to put on a brave face as the "experienced traveler." I had been to Durban once by train as a teenage boy about 10 years prior.

Though Sue was scared, she was also excited to see this new city that she had heard so much about. It would be the first time in her life that she would get to see the crashing waves of the beautiful Indian Ocean, and even though she was afraid I could see a glimmer of adventure in her eyes. After the long overnight train ride in the second class compartment, the train finally pulled into the station in Durban. It was a beautiful Autumn morning and we could smell the ocean in the warm humid air. My mum's brother, uncle Mundie, met us at the train station and took us to his home in Merebank where he, his wife, and 10 daughters warmly welcomed two more with Durban hospitality, which included a spicy and delectable curry and rice. That night we slept well, looking forward to new adventures that lie ahead.

Durban proved itself a stunning beach-front metropolis. Though the government tried to move Indians away from the beachfront, about a mile away from the beach, Grey Street still boasted a bustling and vibrant enclave of Indian bazaars and businesses evidenced by the presence everywhere of Indian stores, Indian music, and the compelling aroma of delicious Indian food emanating from the restaurants and marketplace. Our hunger peaked as we saw food vendors scoop out the inside of a half loaf of bread, fill it with steaming hot chicken, or mutton and potato curry, then top it with a sprig of cilantro and accentuate the dish with a fresh carrot salad. "That's a bunny chow!" my uncle exclaimed, and laughed at the thought that us "Jo'burgers" had never tasted one before. As we peered through the little store windows at all the sweet treats, our eyes would always fall on the bright orange little spirals of jelebee, a slightly crunchy sweet treat, dripping with syrupy goodness.

People had accents different from those in the Transvaal; some spoke with a slang which sounded unfamiliar, while others, obviously well educated, spoke with Oxford accented English. Among them were Zulus, a smattering of so-called "Coloureds" (people of mixed race origin) and Whites, who generally spoke only English.

As we shopped, an older white man looked at me straight in the eye and clearly calling me by my name, "Sammy" he said "How much are the green beans?" I was dumbfounded. How did he know my name? Before I could reply, the owner of the vegetable stand quickly answered on my behalf, "One rand a pound, Sir." I quickly went over to ask my uncle if he knew this strange white man because he somehow knew my name. My uncle could barely breathe as he tried in vain to contain his laughter. "We are all Sammy to the Vellaikaara (Tamil for white person)." This was when I learned that most white people who shopped at Indian stores could not pronounce Indian names and referred to Indians disdainfully as "Sammy" and "Mary." I joked with my uncle that I was happy that they all knew my name.

After our first few days with the Mundie family, on the Tuesday after the long weekend, I went to meet my colleague, a South African born Englishman who was very proud of his heritage, his English history. He nostalgically recalled his fore-parents who subjugated India and made it "British East India" for centuries. He boasted of his South African connection to the Crown Colony in the name of the British Queens Victoria and Elizabeth with King George and his infamous cohorts. One of my colleague's known trademarks was that of being "brutally frank" and he made it known that he did not "beat around the bush, but called a spade, a spade." However, he did not like it when I became frank with him. I learned that this was his modus operandi; proud to be viewed as frank, but not able to allow reciprocation of such, especially from a person of color. He made it certainly clear that as an Englishman, he was proud of his people who knew how to rule and had done so for centuries in different parts of the world. "The sun never sets on the British Empire," he would pridefully declare.

I was a fellow minister assigned to a mission in Durban to start new churches in the surrounding Indian areas. My afore-mentioned mentor and superintendent, decided to take me to lunch at the home of another English couple, who were working in Natal. As we neared the area, the streets became more pristine with tree-lined broad paved roads. The car pulled up to a big beautiful house with perfectly manicured gardens, situated not far from the beach, and rolled to a stop. My colleague immediately alighted from the car and quickly opened my door. He took me by my arm, leading me ostensibly through the side gate of the house, to the back door, where he seated me at the kitchen table. The back door was normally reserved for use by the servants. He then joined the white couple in the living room where they engaged in hearty conversation. I noticed their big dog enter the front door and join them on the comfortable couch in the living room. As the wife stood up to set up the dining room table for a scrumptious lunch, I overheard my mentor quietly tell her that she could serve me lunch at the kitchen table.

Though hungry, I politely declined to eat. In fact, I was ready to leave quietly through the kitchen door, but the big dog, in the backyard now, looked more vicious than when he was reclining on the sofa earlier. Also, I knew that walking down the street in a white area, was not a good idea for a person of color, so I sat there waiting for them to finish so I could leave when they were ready to go. When my hosts finally realized that I was not eating, their conversation came to an abrupt end and they guiltily tried their best to get me to join them in the dining room. I declined their repeated invitations and cajoling.

My own frame of mind as a very young pastor was like that of most South Africans of color at that time. You never questioned authority, namely, the white man, and you never talked back to the white man. You could lose your job or be placed in serious disfavor with the controlling power in your life, and that of the country. Worse yet, any white person could report you to the police with allegations of an obstinate and subversive person of color that is opposed to the governing system. Needless to say, I returned home very troubled that people who claimed to be my "brothers" could act in this manner.

A few weeks after we had moved into a little home in Durban, right next door to my uncle's home, we returned some borrowed items like pots, pans, cups, plates and cutlery, to the white missionary and his wife. They told us that we could have kept these items longer, as they belonged to the "maid," who was on leave. We had much in common with the maid, usually Black or Indian in Durban, but were surprised again that those who called us "brother" and "sister" displayed that brotherly love, so shamefully. Were separate utensils indeed necessary for the maid, who took care of their every need, better than that of her very own family?

A few months later I received an invitation to visit a white church at Morningside in Durban, with a pastor who assured me that I would have "special" seating, which I knew meant segregated seating. I declined the invitation, and told him in the presence of his wife and mine, that I had decided not to have anything to do with the "white church," because of the aforementioned blatant incident of racism. Both he and his wife quickly blamed the South African government for their ghastly behavior. They never apologized but offered excuses, "We were afraid that the police would raid the house and charge us for having you sit in the home." I had tried to protect my young wife from this shameful experience. Upon hearing it right then for the first time, she was supportive of me and mortified at the same time. I then told them about the remainder of the day that I had visited with them.

Instead of driving me back to my home in the Indian neighborhood, as planned, the superintendent dropped me in the city at night in a very dangerous neighborhood. He left me to fend for myself because he was running late for a dinner that he was attending. I took the non-white bus with a sign to my Indian area, but became increasingly concerned when I could not recognize any of the stops. As I reluctantly climbed off the bus at the last stop, the driver asked if I were new to the area. When I affirmed, he told me to remain on the bus as this was a very dangerous neighborhood. He then drove me to Clarewood, stopped another bus, and asked the driver who appeared to be his friend, to drop me close to my home address, 98 Nizam Road in Merebank, as he handed me back my bus fare. To my surprise, the second bus driver, drove me off his route, directly to my home. He refused to accept the fare that had been returned to me by the first, kind-hearted bus-driver. These two drivers were likely of a different religious affiliation than mine. I am always so thankful to God that he sent the right people to cross my path when I needed them most. They took care of me when my Christian brothers left me by the roadside.

The bus drivers epitomized the Good Samaritan that we read about in Luke 10:30-37.

> *Jesus said: "A man was going down from Jerusalem to Jericho, when he was attacked by robbers. They stripped him of his clothes, beat him and went away, leaving him half dead. A priest happened to be going down the same road, and when he saw the man, he passed by on the other side. So too, a Levite, when he came to the place and saw him, passed by on the other side. But a Samaritan, as he traveled, came where the man was; and when he saw him, he took*

pity on him. He went to him and bandaged his wounds, pouring on oil and wine. Then he put the man on his own donkey, brought him to an inn and took care of him. The next day he took out two denarii and gave them to the innkeeper. 'Look after him,' he said, 'and when I return, I will reimburse you for any extra expense you may have.' "Which of these three do you think was a neighbor to the man who fell into the hands of robbers?" The expert in the law replied, "The one who had mercy on him." Jesus told him, "Go and do likewise."

The leaders challenged me to go, like Abraham, who left his homeland, trekking through the dry arid desert from Ur of the Chaldees. He did not count the cost and did not know where he was going, but God blessed him and provided for all his needs. Being a young new Christian, a recent college graduate, fired-up and inspired by the words quoted from the bible, I decided to go, in spite of the risk.

The holy men who had left all in their homeland to come to the mission field in "darkest Africa" to sacrifice for Christ prayed for me. In the actual words of one of them, "Go to Durban and start a church, like Abraham. Do not worry about anything, just rig up with soap boxes a kitchen table and chairs; sleep on a mat on the floor until God provides for your needs. God is faithful, He will take care of you." Only later when I read my bible more intensely did I discover that Abraham was a rich man and had flocks and herds of cattle, and an army of about three hundred men.

We wondered how these "poor" leaders managed to drive

big cars, live in sizable homes and spend holidays on the beaches. There were some who were truly compassionate and did sacrifice much for others. However, many easily succumbed to this system and accepted the benefits of being white, which included a higher pay scale for the same work. My full salary would not be enough to pay for gas for their cars or to buy food for their pets. How would we rent in Durban and pay for food and other expenses, when our salary was only sufficient for some meals? I marvel today that we survived and did not die of starvation. My wife did get ill, seriously. I attribute her illness to the fumes emitted constantly from the oil refineries nearby, and the pressures of hunger and poverty.

Because of the Group Areas Act, enacted to separate the races in South Africa, Indians, brought by the British from India as indentured laborers to work on the region's vast sugarcane plantations, were confined in cities further inland, away from the tropical paradise. Indian towns such as Merebank and Chatsworth, were filled with smoke all day and night from nearby oil refineries. The tomato factory, also close by, spewed the stench of rotten residue, into the pristine Indian Ocean air. During our 2-3 year stay in Durban, Sue developed asthma and almost died after several hospitalizations. This gave impetus for our return to Johannesburg. We bid farewell to our family and new church family, including the Massey's and Gena Peters, amazing young people who later became leaders in the church and in their communities. The three young churches there would later be led by Rev. Porthan and Rev. Subjee, wonderful young men from our Johannesburg ministry. Sadly, we grieved over the years, as many of my uncle's 10 daughters developed and died from unknown lung conditions. My beautiful cousins, our gracious hosts when we arrived in Durban!

What was even more disconcerting was that when we left Johannesburg, we had only a few rands (like the dollar, 1 rand equals 100 cents) for spending in my wallet. I feel deeply embarrassed to even mention the amount. My meager salary of R35.00 (thirty five rands), would only be paid at the end of the month. Today, when I think about this, I wonder how on earth could I have subjected my young bride and myself to this kind of deprivation.

We realize God's people may fail us but God never fails. None of us are perfect. We are all sinners by nature, but God's grace is sufficient for us. Though painful, these experiences have made us stronger, and more sensitive to others. We have forgiven, and are glad that some have returned to ask for forgiveness.

Sadly, we faced this kind of treatment very frequently and many others did as well. After the aforementioned experience, when I had to stop by the home of these colleagues to take care of some church matters, I decided not to enter their home, but to wait outside. I assured them that despite their treatment of me, they would always be welcome in my home, by way of my front door.

Application Approval for South African born children of color (in this case Priscilla and Susheela our daughters aged 3 and 2) to move from Natal, back to Johannesburg, Transvaal, across Provincial (State) Lines.

Sam and Sue with Priscilla and Susheela in Durban.

4

DOUBLE DOSE OF DEFIANCE

by Melanie Moonsamy
daughter of Samuel and Sue Moonsamy

EARLY each morning I would watch Big-Huma (dad's mom) get up from the bed we shared. Though small in stature, we fondly referred to her as Big-Huma because she was the older of the two grandmas. In South African culture, the older you are, the more respect you gain. Huma in the Indian language of Tamil, was a term for mom/grandma. Quietly and methodically she would pleat and drape a sari around her full-length under-skirt, then deftly loop it up and over one shoulder. I always marveled at how quickly she could transform six yards of sheer fabric into a beautiful, long flowing dress. Just as quickly, she would knot her hair into a low bun, revealing the pretty earrings she never ever removed. A simple woman, with meager possessions, her earrings, which

27

looked like round flowers with rubies for petals, were likely her most valuable possession, probably her dowry. After quickly dressing, she would be ready for all that the new day would bring.

Our two grandmas totally contrasted each other in many ways, yet shared a similar inner strength. Big-Huma, dad's mom, lived with us and helped care for all six of us during the week when mom and dad had to work. Small-Huma, mom's mom, wore pretty flowing dresses, her long black hair in large, dramatic curls, with red lipstick and big shiny earrings, of course not the norm for a woman in that day and age. She attended special events, like weddings, in glittering saris. I have pieced together stories about both of our grandmothers and it goes like this ...

As a young woman, Small-Huma would turn heads when she walked down the street. She was vibrant and beautiful. A friend secretly mailed her picture to a beauty competition, and she was surprised to receive a train ticket in the mail to Cape Town to receive her prize. She had won the beauty competition and was in disbelief. Not only was she already a mother of five, albeit a very young mother, but the idea of an Indian woman winning a beauty pageant in that day and age in South Africa, was ludicrous! She was overjoyed and started packing right away.

Her mother-in-law could not believe the audacity of her daughter-in-law. How on earth could she have the gall to go to a strange city to accept an award, let alone a beauty pageant award? Could she not stay home like other decent housewives? Her husband was youthful and handsome after all, and had overcome many obstacles to excel in business. Couldn't the daughter-in-law appreciate the prosperity and opportunity provided by her husband?

The young mother's excitement could not be dampened and she left to claim her prize, despite the strong disapproval of her husband and mother-in-law. Certainly, they would not make good on all of their angry threats, particularly the threat that if she left without permission to redeem her prize, her husband would be married to a more agreeable second wife. She knew that he loved her too much and would never do such a thing. Part of the prize included a cash award. Certainly this would please them, she thought.

She eventually arrived in the beautiful city of Cape Town, approximately a thousand miles from home right at the Southern tip of Africa, where the majestic Indian and Atlantic oceans meet. Her friend that had mailed in that winning picture, accompanied her. With nervous anticipation, she arrived at the hotel to claim her prize and meet the esteemed selection committee. To her dismay, after meeting her, some of the committee members quietly ushered her into a side-room and explained that they were sorry about the confusion. They had chosen her based on a black and white photograph and did not realize that she was not white. They offered her a small amount of the prize money for the inconvenience and quickly and privately dismissed her. Deeply embarrassed, she and her friend quietly left the pageant. She arrived home after a long train journey to another shocking discovery; her husband had indeed been hurriedly married to another woman. Rejected and ashamed, she packed her things and took her 5 children with her to a new life of poverty. Though her husband later begged for her forgiveness and tried to win her back, she would not succumb. She had her pride, and therefore refused to accept a penny from him, not even for food or clothing for their children. They had to now learn how to live a different life, a life of riches to rags.

Dad's mom, big-huma, would always stretch the little she had, to meet the needs of her 9 children. Though small in stature, she always displayed immense courage and protected her family fiercely. On one occasion, she got tired of listening to a neighbor brag about his high caste family. She responded, "Do you see my dog over there? His name is Tiger and he is also high caste." She swiftly walked off leaving the neighbor to continue his conversation with the high caste dog.

On another occasion, the police were terrorizing the neighborhood, hunting for "undocumented domestic laborers" (though they were born in South Africa). They banged loudly on our door and demanded, "Is there a 'girl' working here?" Big-Huma stared at them with fiery eyes and said, "I am a girl and I work in this home." We children held our breaths wondering what they would say or do to our beloved Big-Huma. Even as kids, we had seen the horror of police brutality. To our surprise, the two big, burly police officers at our door, looked at each other, sighed, shook their heads in resignation, and simply walked away. We gasped a sigh of relief and were so glad that they did not further harass our grandmother.

Just two years after our arrival in California in 1987, we were blessed to have Big-Huma, Small-Huma, and my dad's dear Uncle Mundie, come to visit us. This was the first plane trip for mom's mom, and dad's mom had just taken one short flight from Johannesburg to Durban previously. They were extremely nervous, but with much coaxing from all of us, agreed to make this long journey to see us.

At the first USA port of entry in Seattle, they inquired from others on the plane if this was America. Tired from the long journey, they were so relieved to be in America, and quickly disembarked. Several minutes later, they were found walking toward the baggage claim, by an out-of-breath flight attendant.

She looked for them frantically, because the plane was about to continue on to San Francisco, when it was discovered that three passengers were missing. My dad had sent a letter to the airline before their departure, kindly requesting assistance for the three senior travelers.

As their plane landed in San Francisco, we excitedly waited, with flowers and balloons, to welcome them. We patiently watched as the passengers and flight crew coursed through the doors. With still no sight of them, we were becoming increasingly nervous now because the whole area had quieted down after the steady stream of arrivals, and we were the only family still waiting. Eventually, a customs officer came out, smiled at us and said, "You must be waiting for the three elderly travellers?" "Yes, are they okay?" He told us that they were just fine but were arguing with customs officials about the curry leaves that had been confiscated from their luggage. They had purchased these aromatic herbs for my mom's curry and did not want to give them up. With relief that they were okay, we told the customs officer to give them a message from us, to please leave the curry leaves as we were eager to see them.

Then they finally appeared. What a beautiful emotional, reunion! On the three hour drive from the San Francisco International Airport to Yuba City, California, we heard about how Small-Huma had bought, dried, and neatly packed the fragrant curry leaves that, at the time, we could not get in California. Mom tried to explain to them that plants were prohibited by customs, but both grandmas were totally convinced that the immigration officers had intentionally kept the curry leaves for personal use.

Sometimes I wonder if I have been blessed with a double-dose of defiance in my genes, directly passed down from my two Humas.

"Small" Huma (Sue's mom)   "Big" Huma (Sam's mom)

5

MACHADODORP

told by Samuel Moonsamy
written by his daughter Susheela Moonsamy

SUE and I got the car loaded with our luggage and all six kids, and we were on our way to the Eastern Transvaal, home of the world famous Kruger National Park, a wild animal park with an area of about 7500 square miles, and an amazing array of wild African animals. It was the Summer month of December, the Christmas holiday season. Though we hoped to visit Kruger Park, the primary purpose of the trip was to attend the annual Campus Crusade for Christ (CCC) Conference which would give us the time to get away from home and spend time with fellow staff members, as we studied the bible, shared, learned, and grew together.

CCC was a group that we joined after we had made the decision to leave our church, a church that did not want to

risk offending the South African government and the laws of
Apartheid, laws that were clearly contrary to the law of God.
It was a difficult decision to leave our church as we had built
strong relationships over many years, particularly with many
of the ministers, some who had attended bible college with me.
The new interdenominational group impressed us because
they insisted on equality and non-segregation, despite the
laws that were still in effect in the early eighties in South Africa.
This conference was one of the few non-segregated events
we attended in South Africa with our entire family. The kids
enjoyed this time as it was like a vacation for them; they got
to make new friends and attend all the fun activities planned
for them. After traveling for half a day on this scenic route,
we eventually arrived at our destination, a beautiful secluded
resort-type conference center, nestled in the mountains of
the Eastern Transvaal, surrounded by lush green trees. The
nearest city was about 50 miles away.

On the second or third night of the conference, Sue presented a dynamic talk about her life experiences and her journey of faith, bringing many to tears. Late that very night,
Sue suddenly took ill. She started getting headaches and kept
taking painkillers, to no avail. The headaches continued and
seemed to worsen. Finally, one of our colleagues, a resident
medical student, checked Sue's symptoms and told me to get
her to the nearest hospital as soon as possible. He suspected
meningitis. By this time, she was experiencing severe, unbear-
able pain. We got her into the car and were off to the closest
non-white hospital where she was immediately admitted. After a lumbar puncture (spinal tap), she was diagnosed with en-
cephalitis, which is an inflammation of the brain, most-likely
contracted through a mosquito-bite. We were devastated and
prayed for her healing with many others at the conference.

She spent the rest of the week in the hospital while we stayed at the conference grounds not knowing what to do. This was a very rural area and we were praying that she would recover sufficiently to be able to travel back home. I asked the doctor if she could be released so that we could get her home, but he said that she was not well enough to travel. At the end of the conference we pleaded with the doctor and he finally agreed to release her from the hospital, a night before our departure home. Prior to making the long drive the following day, with Sue on a makeshift bed on the back seat of our van (combi), we stopped by the hospital once more, and the doctor had to come out to the car to give her a shot before the trip, as she was too weak to get out of the vehicle to go back into the hospital. We decided to immediately drive back home. I asked one of our colleagues, who was a close friend, if he and his family would follow us as we drove home. Praying as we left the conference site, we drove down the beautiful scenic route again, which this time seemed grim as we were all so worried about Sue who appeared to be at her worst, on this day.

After traveling for about two hours, winding our way up to the top of a steep hill our eight seater van suddenly started coughing up gusts of white smoke, leaving plumes and trails of white clouds behind us. The kids became anxious and afraid, since they thought the car was on fire. Our son Neil, about 8 years old at the time, yelled out, "let's get out of here before the car explodes!" In the distance, I managed to spot a gas station up at the top of the hill; I knew and believed that I could make it to the top. By this time Sue was so ill that she had become delirious and was unaware of this grave situation. The van panted to the top of the hill and as we rolled into the gas station, the VW van gave a few more huffs and puffs and completely stalled. The combi/van would not respond to my repeated attempts to try and restart her. I looked over to my right and saw a AAA car which is known as "AA (Automobile Association)" in South Africa. I asked the AAA technician if he would help me and in an uncouth way, with no regard for my children, he shouted with expletives that there was nothing he could do for us since the car's engine was messed up. Thank God that the Valentine family, who had followed us all the way, was right there with us. Terry immediately offloaded most of his family's luggage from their station wagon, so that they could lower the back seat to make room for Sue to lie down. We then transferred her to Terry and Priscilla Valentine's car. Our oldest daughter, also named Priscilla, accompanied her mom as they rushed home so that Sue could get medical attention.

I then went into the gas station and explained to the gentleman behind the counter what had happened and asked if I could please use the telephone to call for some help. He bluntly refused. Then reality hit; though coming from a non-segregated conference, I was left all alone with a broken down vehicle to fend for five of my six children, in a conservative white town called Machadodorp, in South Africa during the height of Apartheid, while my gravely ill wife was being rushed home for emergency medical treatment. I thought to myself, "What do I do next?" In a state of total helplessness, I looked up to the sky and said, "God you have always been with me and I know that only you will protect us and give me direction in this situation." As I lowered my head and looked down from the top of the hill at the town that lay spread out at the foot of this hill, my eye immediately fell on a steeple, a church steeple. I quickly asked a young man who was leaving the gas station at that time if he could give me a ride to that church below. Fortunately he was willing to do so, but only had space for one. I told the kids to lock the doors and remain in the car with the luggage and reassuringly said to them "I will be back shortly." When I look back I cringe that I had to leave them in the hot lowveld sun in the car, in such a hostile, unfriendly environment, but I was helpless with no other alternative but to desperately seek help for my family.

Not knowing where I was going, I prayed again as we drove all the way down to the bottom of the hill directly to the church. I was glad when I immediately noticed the parsonage next door to the church, but at the same time I felt fearful, as I also noticed that this happened to be a Dutch Reformed Church, which strictly adhered to the South African system of racial segregation during that time. The young man who had given me a ride had already left, so I had no choice now but to go up to the door. I nervously rang the doorbell not knowing what to expect. The door opened, and I was greeted by a woman who asked what I wanted. She told me that she was the wife of the "Dominee," which is the Afrikaans term for "pastor" in the White South African, Afrikaans language. I explained to her in Afrikaans that our vehicle had broken down, and I needed to use a telephone to call for some help to get us home to my wife who was seriously ill. To my surprise she invited me in, and wanted to know more about what had happened, where the children were, and where the car was. Her husband came in and together they both wanted to know if everyone was okay. They allowed me to use the telephone and then Dominee Henk Theron quickly drove me back up to the gas station where the vehicle and kids were. He loaded his station-wagon with all of our luggage, plus the extra luggage that we had to take out of the Valentine's car, and our five remaining kids. We were packed tighter than sardines in a can with luggage all around us ready to depart. This kind, gentle dominee did not even mind overloading his vehicle, and to our surprise and amazement, Dominee Theron drove us all the way home, approximately 250 miles that afternoon. I was overcome with emotion as we traveled along, listening to the beautiful choruses he played in his car. The kids enjoyed some delicious sandwiches and fruit that his wife, Mrs Flippie Theron had hurriedly prepared, before we left for our trip home.

We reached home that night and were glad to see that Sue had arrived home earlier and had been treated by our local doctor, Dr Budhia, who so kindly made a house call, and was leaving as we arrived. In addition, Sue's cousin Manor Moodley was there to welcome us with a warm meal. Dominee Theron came in, prayed with Sue, and then left back home. He refused any money for gas and needed to head back home to attend a meeting the following day, though we offered for him to stay overnight. He told me not to worry about our van, as he would have it towed to a garage, where it could be repaired. A few days later, I went back up to Machadodorp to pick up the van. I pulled out my credit card to pay the bill and found that Dominee Theron had arranged for the engine to be replaced and had paid the entire bill. He refused any repayment! I was more than amazed by the warmth and love we received from a total stranger in a conservative white town where this was not expected at all. He was not afraid of endangering his life by going out of his way to help our family.

I did not know what to do to thank this kind, thoughtful couple, since they had refused any type of payment. I decided to contact the local newspaper in Machadodorp, and wrote a letter of thanks to be published in the newspaper, to show our appreciation, and at the same time, to make the people in the town aware of what a remarkable dominee they had. After the article was published, Dominee Theron called me to let me know that his church was full of new locals who were so overcome by his act of kindness. I was then contacted by several of the larger newspapers including the Sunday Times, that asked if they could publish this story, as they felt that since it was December, this was a beautiful Christmas story of love and peace at a time when the country was experiencing racial hatred and strife.

Sue struggled through weeks and months of severe illness, the most difficult days were when she could not even recognize her own family, due to the inflammation of her brain. The doctors said that even if she recovered, she would most likely be blind, lose her hearing, or not be able to walk. I clearly remember our daughter Priscilla sobbing when her mom did not recognize her. On another day, she found her mom trying to read the bible while holding it upside-down. I remember when the news reporter came to interview us, Sue was having a good day, and she attempted to walk outside. Our two oldest girls, Priscilla and Susheela, immediately rushed to each side of their mom, pretending not to be overly concerned, but just waiting to catch her if necessary. Sue smiled and asked them, "Don't you believe that God is healing me." From that moment, she never needed help walking again. Sue recovered completely from her illness and was able to return to her normal way of life.

We are so thankful for all of the prayer and support we received during that difficult time. We remember how a friend set up a telephone prayer chain where a prayer was started by one call and then continued by friends and family throughout South Africa and even around the world. We are especially thankful to God for Sue's restoration of health, and for the people who touched our lives in such a remarkable way, particularly in this tiny little town called Machadodorp in the Eastern

Transvaal in South Africa.

After a long search, we recently found contact information and called the Theron home. Mrs. Flippie Theron remembered us and told us that her husband, the dominee had died in a tragic motor accident a few years ago. We were saddened to hear this news but assured her that we will always be grateful to her and her husband for their true "Good Samaritan," compassionate love.

We recently learned that the name of the little town of Machadodorp has been changed to eNtokozweni, which translates to … a place of happiness.

6

SUE'S STORY

told by Sue Moonsamy
written by her children Neil and Ursula Moonsamy

I finally began to listen to my mother, as she reached under the sink and took out a gallon of paraffin (kerosene). My mother had been quietly crying all day and started to sob as she rambled on, "..the boys will be okay...but...but, this life is just too hard for girls." Expecting my mother to walk over and fill one of the lamps, or the primus stove, before we even realized what she was about to do, my mother doused my younger sister and me with half of the gallon of kerosene, pouring the rest on herself. It was only then that I realized what my mom was about to do. I could not believe what was happening and I completely froze. I couldn't breathe, I couldn't run, I couldn't scream. My younger sister, only 7 or 8 years old, clutched me tightly. "It's gonna be okay my children" my mother said. It was as if time was standing still as my mother's trembling hand took a match out of the box. As my younger sister screamed "Oh, God!" in desperation, I tightly shut my eyes, and my life flashed before me.

I was born in the non-white town of Lady Selbourne outside the city of Pretoria, the administrative Capital of South Africa, where Apartheid was stringently applied and almost everybody spoke more Afrikaans than English. Here, a minority of Indians lived in two or three mixed communities together with "Coloureds," Blacks, and Chinese. As always, the main city and suburbs were reserved only for Whites.

My personal struggle and pain coincided with the introduction of a new and most feared word known in the world, Apartheid: the total, complete, and comprehensive separation of the races. Separation began in my own home with my parents. The pain and shame of suddenly being without a father in the home was unheard of and unacceptable at that time, particularly within our community. When my friends asked, we were told to say that my father was away at work. To remove herself from the shame she felt in her community, my mom decided to move from Pretoria with her children, Ramie, Thachie, Anand, Sue and Sylvie to another mixed community within the municipal area of Johannesburg, called Sophiatown.

Life in our new environment was exciting. Sophiatown, a crime-ridden community, had here and there a street light in working order, pot-holed streets, and little to no police protection. On Fridays and Saturdays the street corners were alive with spontaneous dancing as someone played the penny whistle, a little flute-like instrument, late into the night and the early parts of the following morning. Like Harlem, New York, or Oakland, California, the eclectic Sophiatown produced artists to the world stage, such as Miriam Makeba and

Hugh Masekela as well as poets, authors, and anti-Apartheid activists. Sophiatown was lined with little shops, and not one, but two movie theaters. It was an exciting town to live in and I loved it.

We moved into one of the units in the backyard of a home with a small kitchen attached. The two-roomed unit had no electricity or running water. There was an outhouse and a faucet outside that was shared with other tenants living in the same yard. We collected our water in a large metal bucket that was left on our coal stove to warm for the day. We would scoop out warm water when needed. At the end of the day the remaining water was put into a tub on the kitchen floor so us kids could enjoy a warm bath; the water soon turned brown as mom put one kid after the other in the same bath. We huddled together in the cold winters on two beds, one for my brothers and one for me, my sister, and my mom. Sometimes there was no wood or coal to make a fire to warm the house.

Unlike our previous home, this outhouse was equipped with the most wonderful modern luxurious amenity we had ever experienced: a flushing toilet. Above the toilet was a tank with a rusty old chain that you would pull to flush. Wedged behind the plumbing was a stack of newspaper; though it was too dark and dank in the little brick room to read. Toilet paper was another luxury that only the wealthy could afford, so we used newspaper. Even though the shared toilet was often clogged, it was much better than the smelly bucket toilets that we had endured in the past.

We tried our best to help my mother out as much as we could. My older brothers were a bit mischievous and figured out all kinds of ways to get by. I remember them sticking chewed gum onto a long stick. They would go to a particular store that kept the coins in a large can behind the counter.

My brother would ask for a particular oil that he knew was in the back room, and when the store owner went to the back he would quickly use the homemade contraption to fish some money out of the can. When the store owner returned, he would use the same money he had just stolen to pay for the oil. Depending on how much he was able to steal, he would add some other items, like candy.

I attended Sophiatown Primary (Elementary) School for three years, then moved to a school in Newclare. I would walk with my friends Stephanie and Selma a long way, about a mile and a half through Western Native Township to get to school. It was suddenly deemed inappropriate for Indians to attend school in Newclare, as it was now declared a Coloured area. Selma and I were bussed to Lenasia Primary, later known as Alpha Primary, in the new township of Lenasia, allocated just for Indians. We missed going to school with our close friend Stephanie whom we fondly called Stevie.

While I loved school, my brother Anand, though very intelligent, hated school and often played truant. On one occasion when he was absent, the teacher sent some of his classmates to our home to bring him to school. He hid from these kids by quickly climbing into the ceiling. He stayed there quietly listening for them to leave. Suddenly the ceiling gave way and with a loud bang, he fell through. Realizing that his classmates were still there, he landed feet first onto the bed and catapulted behind the closet (wardrobe). When the kids ran into the room to see where the noise had come from, they saw a big hole in the ceiling with dust streaming down, and no sign of my brother. They assumed that he had jumped out of the open window and had run away. After they left, we could not control our laughter as we saw him slowly crawl out from behind the closet, his head and face covered in white ceiling dust, with large peering eyes, embarrassedly looking back at us.

Like all children, we loved school holidays … except this particular time. My brothers were away at my grandmother's home in Pretoria while my young aunt Madhoori, about my age, was with us for a few days. We were in the kitchen one morning when I saw my little sister, only around 7 years of age, topple the boiling kettle of water over herself. She gasped trying to extricate herself from this traumatic occurrence, but it was too late. We could see the damage resulting in huge blisters, as we lifted her clothing.

Little Sylvia, whom we nicknamed Sylvie, was in excruciating, mind-wrecking pain, writhing in my arms. In that moment I was beside myself, panic-stricken, not knowing what to do while she lay helpless, crying. Because it was the morning of a school holiday, mom was at work and so were the few people who owned cars in our neighborhood. Our only option was to carry Sylvia in our arms, and walk to the nearest non-white hospital, Coronation Hospital, a good two miles away.

My young aunt, Madhoori, was born with only one arm. She and I took turns carrying the scalded child. We switched at every light pole. "Don't cry Sylvie. We'll be at the hospital soon," I said to her as we laid her alongside the road on the grass to take a little bit of a rest. Pitifully moaning and groaning, at times she lay still, as if she were dead. Then like out of a cloud, a slowly trotting horse and cart approached. "Oupa, Please Help Us!" I screamed. The old man immediately stopped and helped us to climb on to the back of his cart. "Oupa," which means grandfather, is an Afrikaans term of respect for an older man. All the way as we travelled, Sylvia cried on the shaking cart. Relieved, we reached the hospital with the help of this angel with his horse and cart.

Sylvie received medical treatment. The next morning Madhoori and I, returned with Sylvia to the hospital. We sat among rows of people in the casualty section, and waited to be seen by a doctor. Finally about noon we were about to see the doctor when to our horror, I discovered that I had left the hospital card at home. "Where's your card?" the orderly asked. I fumbled through my pockets. There was no card. "We must have left it at home," I said. "Please sir, allow us to see the doctor. My sister is very ill and our home is so far away."

All our begging and crying did not change his mind. He remained adamant and insisted that we go home and bring the card. We struggled for several hours to walk home. By this time the wounds in her body were festering, blood was beginning to seep through the bandage, and she was running a fever.

A neighbor happened to be at home, when we got there. He was shocked when he saw Sylvie's condition and rushed to get her immediate emergency treatment. He loaded us into his car and knowing that there would be long lines at the hospital, he decided that he would take us nearby to a doctor whom he knew, in fact, a dentist!

Seeing the plight of a little girl in dire need and distress, the dentist decided to dress the wounds and administer whatever medication he had. He did this out of compassion as he realized Sylvia's serious situation. He also called the hospital and gave them a strict warning to take care of her and her wounds. They promised to comply, because he threatened to report them. Sylvie's leg was so badly burned that doctors were considering an amputation, but through the grace of God, after much pain and with time, she recovered fully.

To support the family, my mom worked in a clothing factory for eight or more hours a day, in sweatshop conditions, with minimal remuneration. Most of the time she came home with a loaf of bread. In most cases, we ate plain bread, but sometimes mom would also provide a small piece of butter bought from a local Chinese store. Butter was a luxury and mom had to always hear the squabbling between us kids, "you got more butter than I did." When she did bring food home to prepare, she was a fantastic cook.

When I was just thirteen years old, my mom found me a job in a factory. I had to leave school and wear make-up and shoes with a little heel, so I could appear older. I worked as a "nipper" at the dress factory, cutting excess threads to neaten newly sewn school uniforms, uniforms that I should have been wearing at the time.

Eventually, to my delight, my dear friends Stevie and Selma came to work at the factory with me. One of the kind elderly ladies who worked with us must have noticed that we were younger than the 16 year olds we claimed to be, and asked why we were working and not at school. Stevie replied that she did not have a father. I quickly responded that my father had died too.

We would merrily skip and hop home together each day, giggling as most teenage girls would. We always stopped and looked at the mouth-watering food at a hamburger place between the factory and the bus-stop in the city of Johannesburg. We had never been in a restaurant in our lives before. It was a long wait to the end of the month, when we would eventually get our wages. The three of us excitedly decided that we would use a little bit of our pay at the end of the month to finally eat in this restaurant that we passed by each day.

The day had finally come. We walked in and sat on the tall

stools at the counter, excited to finally order the delicious food we had been eyeing all month. Ready to place the first order, just as we had rehearsed, from behind the counter we suddenly heard a stern voice shouting loudly at us in Afrikaans: "Ja, wat soek julle? Uit! uit! Julle moet uit gaan, voor ek die polisie roep!" (Yes, what do you want in here? Get out, get out, before I call the police!) We immediately ran out in fear. We gathered our composure, and walked home in silence. Eventually we looked at each other and all we could do was laugh. Sometimes we had to laugh to keep our sanity because we had experiences like these often.

Later on, my brother Anand and I worked with my mom at her job. We learned to appreciate my mom so much more. We worked in a large room. Anand was stationed at the far end cutting fabrics, my mom in the middle with many others operating the sewing machines, and I was at the other end snipping off excess threads and folding. My mom told us to never talk to her during work. We sat at our assigned stations all day, and sometimes I would peer over to observe my mom working without stopping; beads of sweat sometimes building up on her brow.

One afternoon, I saw the manager yell at my mom in a condescending manner in front of everyone because she had made a mistake. My heart sank as she embarrassingly apologized and continued her work. On another occasion, a young lady walked away from her station and started a conversation with her friend who kept working while she talked. The manager then called this young lady over the loudspeaker and fired her immediately as an example to all of us.

As we got older, we got to meet our siblings from my dad's second marriage, Savami, Vishnu and Saggie. It is amazing that through my dad we are connected as family for life and that the love and bond grows deeper with time.

One day, my mom gave my brothers money to go and see a movie, which was a rare treat. I begged to tag along because I knew that my idol Elvis Presley had a movie playing at Balansky's theater nearby. I would have given anything in the world to see Elvis Presley. I would take the longer route past the theater just to see his poster plastered on the walls. We would listen to the small transistor radio to hear his songs and listen to his dreamy voice. "Please, please, can I go with," I had begged. My mother replied, "Not today my child, I really need your help at home." My heart sank, and my brother Anand knew exactly what to say to make me feel better, "Don't worry we are not going to see the Elvis movie at Balansky's, that's for girls. We are going to watch a Western at Odin's, you wouldn't wanna see it."

The boys left and Sylvie and I continued to play in the backyard. I peeked inside every now and again to see when my mom needed our help. I noticed my mom was praying and silently crying. I felt sorry for my mom. I knew how hard she worked and how much she wanted to make us all happy. "Are you okay, mommy?" I asked, as I entered the house. "I'm okay my child," she said "come inside." Sylvie and I entered the house and she closed and locked the door behind us. I looked around and noticed that all the curtains were drawn.

...she reached under the sink and took out a gallon of kerosene...she doused my younger sister and me...pouring the rest on herself...I couldn't breathe...I couldn't run...I couldn't scream...my mother's trembling hand took a match out of the box...I tightly shut my eyes.

My little sister screamed in desperation, "Oh God!" We heard a thud on the floor. I opened my eyes, expecting to be engulfed in flames. Instead, my mom was on the floor, match still in hand. She had fainted. I know that God heard and answered my little sister's cry that day. Instinctively, I tried to tend to my mom to see what had happened to her. My little sister tapped me on the shoulder and said, "Let's get out of here!" She reached into mom's pocket and found the key, and we ran to the movie theater to find our brothers.

We waited, disheveled and shivering, outside Odin's Bioscope (Movie Theatre) for my brothers to come out. They were shocked to see us there in this state, and after hearing about our experience, rushed home with us.

When we got home, we were surprised to find my mother in the kitchen preparing dinner as if nothing had happened. She had gotten up, cleaned the house and taken a shower. My oldest brother had a serious talk with her and made her promise that she would never attempt anything like this in the future. We never spoke of this again.

Sylvie and Sue

7

THE STEPHANIE HOTEL

by Samuel Moonsamy

I T was 1950 when I applied for my first job at the Ambassador Hotel in Hillbrow Johannesburg. Though not the best job in town, because of financial pressure, I needed this job as a page-boy (bellman). Within a few days I learned how to work the switchboard, operating the telephone system at the hotel which worked on a cord system. We plugged the cords into the room number on the board as the calls came throughout the day and night.

In any job situation the foreboding fear was not of the job, but how we would be treated by white people who were always, without exception, either the bosses or the supervisors. At this time in the history of South Africa I did not know of any blacks in good positions at any place of employment. Even though it was supposedly against the law for people in control to beat, ill-treat or abuse the workers, this was so common. I heard that the manager of this hotel had kicked a black waiter, who had made a mistake with an order. The waiter simply remained quiet because his job was at stake. Being poor, needy and black meant that you kept your mouth shut and never complained about what white people did to you. If you did complain, it would amount to nothing, for even the police were geared to stand by their white compatriots. Though I was fortunate to never have been assaulted, I was insulted on a few occasions. I was told how stupid we blacks were and often had to listen to people's negative comments about us.

At all times we knew that we had to be polite and courteous on the phone, stand erect when talking to the guests, addressing them as "Sir" or "Madam." However, what was not so easy to understand, was that we had to show the same amount of courtesy and respect to fellow white workers and also refer to them as "Sir" and "Madam."

Here at the Ambassador Hotel, I worked with an Indian young man named Michael. He and I became good friends and remained loyal to each other. At times we had opportunity to become mischievous. His brother Francis, the night porter started work at 10pm, until the next morning. Whenever we worked night shift from 3-10pm it was too late to go home so we would sometimes sleep at the hotel. We would make ourselves comfortable in the lobby with pillows taken from the sofas. For blankets, the only covering available were the tablecloths from the dining room which we replaced before any of the white staff came on duty at 6am in the morning. This offered a great opportunity for us to raid the refrigerators late at night and eat roast chicken, rolls and ice cream and all kinds of delicacies that we could never afford to eat at home.

When we were done with work, we sometimes went home with our tips amounting to about ten shillings, the equivalent of about one dollar and forty cents at the time. I gave all to my mother to purchase the evening meal for the family.

Looking for Another Job

To supplement my income I decided to look for another job in the vicinity of Berea about two miles away and ended up standing at the back gate of the Stephanie Hotel. The guard at the gate quickly whisked me to the office where I met with the manager Mr. Eric Jackson and his wife Maureen. They appeared to be very impressed with me and asked if I could come to work for them immediately. Thinking that I could keep the other job for the day time I responded by telling them that I would like to work in the evenings only. Mrs. Jackson replied: "Oh so you want to go to school in the day time?" "Yes ma'am" I said, though that was not my intention. My intention was merely to earn more money.

Back to School Again

Though making money was important to survive, I realized that getting an education would be more beneficial in the long run. I decided to honor my commitment to go to school. A few days later, I gave notice at the first job. At this new job, I was provided with a carpeted room of my own and clean bedding whenever I wanted. The room in the back of the hotel was separated only by a long passage or hallway leading to the back gate near the garage.

My choice of school was not that easy. Indians had to attend Indian schools by law. Even though the Indian school on

Gold Street was closer, I decided to try again at City and Suburban, the Coloured School that I had previously attended. It felt more comfortable for me, because I had friends there. Previously I stopped attending school there when I became very lethargic due to hunger and lack of sleep. Attending school all day, and working most of the night was difficult, so I played truant often. The principal looked at my birth certificate and saw my name as Subavathie Moonsamy (my Indian name) and immediately asked if the previous student known to them as Samuel Moonsamy was my brother. Fortunately, I was saved by the misapprehension of the principal who thought that Samuel was my brother, when it was, in fact, me. "Yes sir," I replied with much trepidation. His unexpected reply was unmistakably stern and forthright: "If you do as your brother Samuel did, to play truant and not come regularly, I'll ask you to leave and not come back again." So I began my schooling again at City and Suburban Coloured School on Mooi Street near the hotel.

From the Slums Living Like Millionaires

The Jacksons were very kind to me. This was extremely unusual to me. They did not object to me using the white bathroom near the office. They also asked the waiters to bring me a full hotel meal with desserts to the office whenever I worked the night shift. Mrs. Jackson also introduced me as her son to all her guests. I could do my homework in the office, another privilege I enjoyed. Mrs. Jackson checked to see if I did my work regularly. In the mornings when I went to school, she asked the chef in the kitchen to make me a large bag of lunch after I had enjoyed a full hotel breakfast. In the afternoon when I arrived back at work I looked in the huge kitchen ovens and found a full meal; whatever was on the hotel menu for lunch that day, including dessert.

I was from the slums living like a millionaire and eating the best foods like you could only find in a hotel kitchen.

I later recommended my friend Melvin for a job at the hotel; he was of so called "Coloured" descent. He was also hired to work as a switchboard operator, but learned to do all kinds of handyman's work, which included filing of keys, repairing heaters in the winter, and restoring electricity when the light switches tripped.

When Melvin was hired, the fun began. When the electricity short-circuited, he would experiment on the high tension cable box, a job for the electrician, without any fear of electrocution. He also made keys to fit the kitchen fridges and the linen room from which we took new bedding and towels when we wanted. We got into lots of mischief. We phoned the police and connected them to a Chinese store. "Hullo, Marshall Square Police Department. Die polisie Marshal Square." The Chinese businessman replied, "Hello, I did not call the police, what do you want?" This was a lot of fun for us and we laughed a lot whenever we were in the office alone. Today, I cannot believe that we did this. At the time, it was our way of getting even with the police who were usually very stern and abusive. Fortunately for us at that time, technology was not advanced enough to trace the calls to the place of origin.

Later, as time went on, the management changed hands. A man and his wife, from Australia took over. He daily and inadvertently walked by us and sometimes slapped us hard on the head. He acted like he was being playful but we knew he was a racist who hated us and tried everything in his power to make us unhappy and uncomfortable. On some occasions we blocked his hand and at one time he even suffered a sprained wrist for which we were very happy.

The guests at the hotel were mostly Jews, some who had fled Europe during the war and talked in their accents about the war and the suffering of those who were left behind to die in the holocaust. Some Jewish people spent a lot of time talking to us, while others sadly, succumbed quickly to the culture of South Africa, and treated us poorly. In South Africa, Jews were considered part of the 'upper class' white community.

Our monthly salary was seven rands. Later I got an increase to bring my wages up to fifteen rands.

Since Melvin had access to the hotel room keys, the two of us mischievously decided one day that we would use a couple of the hotel rooms to take hot baths since we did not have the luxury of a bath in our own homes. At home we had to fill a large metal tub with water that we got from a well. We heated it in a large metal bucket on the kitchen coal stove so we could take a bath on the kitchen floor. The one mistake Melvin made was to open the linen room to take towels without permission from the boss. One night the boss came knocking on our doors while we were in steaming hot baths. To make things worse, one of these was an old fashioned bath kept mainly as a showpiece near the office. He was very angry with us and ordered us to his office the next day, giving Melvin the sack. Melvin admitted that he had opened the linen room door without permission from the office.

Sometimes I wonder why Melvin was fired and not me. He was the lighter skinned boy with blonde hair and blue eyes, but was classified "Coloured." Melvin called me the very next day from a job he was offered at the newly opened Astor Hotel in the Joubert Park area.

He excitedly asked me to come and visit him at his new job. When I got to the Astor Hotel, Melvin led me up to his room. It was something to behold. The room was carpeted from wall to wall with an en-suite bathroom. It appeared to be brand new and fully furnished. This was a lot better than where I worked. It was a five star guest room with telephone. We could not stop laughing with joy. The Italian manager looking at Melvin felt pity for him, thinking that he was white. For this reason we believe he gave him the very best on an incomplete floor where some of the rooms were still in construction.

Those days it was safe to walk from Joubert Park to Berea, a distance of about 4 miles even at midnight. Coming from the slums of Kliptown, it was like heaven for us to eat the best food and live like kings. We used the telephone profusely and enjoyed communication like the present time. The cost of a telephone call which we got for free, was 3 pennies also known as a "tiekie."

Meeting Nadine Gordimer

Of note at the Stephanie hotel, I got to meet Mrs. Fürstern-burg, an extended-stay resident there. She was a kind lady with a heavy German accent, who introduced me to her grand-daughter, Nadine Gordimer, a budding young writer. Nadine was friendly and gave me an autographed copy of one of her first books. She often came to visit her grandmother at the hotel. I was a little nervous because it was unusual for a white woman to make conversation with non-white staff. Nadine was unafraid to stand at the front desk and have lengthy con-versations with me, asking specific details about life in non-white townships, like Kliptown, where I was living. These conversations occurred many times during the early fifties.

Many years later, in 1991, I was thrilled to hear that Nadine Gordimer became a Nobel Prize Laureate in Literature. I was very inspired by Nadine and hoped that I would somehow have an opportunity to write someday.

Living at Pettycoat Lane near Paardevlei (Parravlei)

In contrast to the luxurious lifestyle at the Stephanie and Astor Hotels, we returned home to Kliptown, a rough town with ramshackle houses. It was a world apart with stark differences. It was an area where Coloureds, Indians and Black South Africans lived together. However, only Coloureds were allowed to buy property here at that time, freehold or leased. Freehold meant that they could own the house as their own but not lease it. Normally, the government leased property or land on a ninety year contract. This meant that if the owner died prior, or lived that long, he would have to relinquish hold on the property when the time period was up, and revert it back to the government.

In between, some of the Indians ran little retail shops named after themselves: Saloojees, Muller's, Khatib's Butchery, a dairy, fruit and grocery shop. The main road leading into the town was dust covered cobblestone and when it rained there was mud and slush all over. No drains were installed so water just seeped into the ground and the residue formed mud puddles everywhere. Without trash cans or bins, ash heaps developed everywhere. The Chinese grocery store sold almost anything from cornmeal, sugar, and meat, to clothing.

"Bansella" was a word we understood and it meant being rewarded with broken cookies or candy for coming to buy at the stores. The store-keeper would shout "Yes, what do you want?" Then after serving the bread and other items which we had bought, he would give us a handful of candy or broken biscuits (cookies), which we delightfully accepted. Cooking oil and paraffin (kerosene) were both commodities bought daily to keep the primus stove (small portable gas stove) working so we could cook.

A bag of coal to make fire was sold at the truck for twenty five cents and a bag of firewood for the same price.

There were, however, little enclaves of houses neatly built. These were minimally adequate with a dining room, a passageway, and the bedroom where all the kids slept, with their parents in the same room. The older ones slept in the dining room or lounge (living room).

Prior to my exposure to life at the hotel, I did not realize how deprived of material possessions we were. However, in my own township, despite the abject poverty, we were respected, accepted, and loved by neighbors, friends, and family. This was unlike the out-of-place feeling in the wealthy environment that I enjoyed at times, but where I had no real sense of belonging. My young mind juggled daily the constant contrast of home and work.

8

THE YOUNG PREACHER'S WIFE

told by Sue Moonsamy
written by her daughters Noelene and Ursula Moonsamy

M Y mother's friend Aunty Mina came to visit us ever so often. We barely realized that Aunty Mina was blind, until she had to be led away from our home again. During one visit she asked my mom if I could lead her to a meeting a few blocks away. My mom agreed. After Aunty Mina left, my mom told me to guide Aunty Mina there and back but to wait outside during the meeting.

The next Sunday, I guided Aunty Mina to her meeting. With her holding onto my arm, we talked and laughed as we walked along the path. It always amazed me how descriptive Aunty Mina was of the world around her, yet she could not see.

When we reached the home, instead of waiting outside as I had planned to do, I became curious and decided to go inside. Nervously I walked into the meeting and was relieved to find warm, smiling faces singing praises to God. After the singing in this little home church, the preacher spoke simply about a God who loved and cared for me. Interested to know this God of love and forgiveness, I prayed and felt a peace that I could not explain.

Around that time, the Group Areas Act passed in 1950, and the South African government started segregating people by race, forcibly moving them from mixed areas like our Sophiatown into racially segregated neighborhoods. Though a rough neighborhood, we loved Sophiatown. Blacks, Coloureds, Indians and Chinese lived in harmony in this vibrant area, and we felt protected by neighbors and friends there. Sophiatown, conveniently located close to the city, boasted a thriving community. There were movie theaters and little stores all within walking distance of our home. With the new laws taking effect in the country, our whole community was now being split apart with people forcefully being moved to areas specified for each classified race group. In strong opposition protesters posted signs everywhere, "WE WILL NOT MOVE." Great leaders such as Trevor Huddleston and Dr AB Xuma stood with the people to resist the forced removals. Large groups gathered, singing freedom songs, and shouting "Ons dak nie, ons phola hier" meaning we will not move we're staying here, a line from the song "Meadowlands" that we heard playing throughout the town. Despite the opposition, approximately 60,000 residents, were eventually forcibly moved out of Sophiatown. In the beginning when the police and army moved people's belongings, they would move back by nightfall. To prevent this from happening, homes were bulldozed as soon as the residents were moved out. Our entire beloved Sophiatown, except for a few prominent structures, was demolished.

At first my family resisted the move. When they realized that they could get me away from my new church and what they termed, "the white man's God," into an all-Indian area, they suddenly decided to go ahead and move to Lenasia. Family housing was not yet developed, so we were moved into barracks at a military camp, that we partitioned with curtains and furniture in the new Indian township of Lenasia.

On our first day there, two young gentlemen visited and talked to my mother. I asked my mother who they were, and she quickly said, "Oh them, don't worry yourself with them, they are just the caretakers. They just stopped by to see if the lights were in working condition." She seemed agitated. I whispered to my sister, "Wow, Lenasia must be some fancy town if the caretakers (custodians) are dressed in suits and ties." Perhaps this area was not going to be so bad after all.

That evening, I sat on the step outside of our unit feeling very sorry for myself. I asked God why he had taken me away from my friends, and the church, that I loved so much. I suddenly heard a song I had recently learned at my house church in Sophiatown, "Trust in the Lord, and don't despair, He is a friend so true." My eyes filled with tears and I thanked God for sending His angels to sing to me. I kept hearing the same song over and over again and it certainly did not sound like angels' voices. A friend from school passed by. I asked her where she was heading, and she said she was going to church at the house next door. I looked at her questioningly as she pointed to the house right next to mine. My mother was in the kitchen listening, as my friend invited me to go with her. I told my friend to wait while I grabbed my sweater. I said "Mom, if you are looking for me, I won't be far away, I'll be right next door." I quickly got out of there, knowing my mother was not amused, and walked with my friend just steps away to the house next door. I entered the home and could not believe my eyes! My mother had moved us from Sophiatown to get me away from a church several blocks away, into the Indian township of Lenasia, with a church right next door!

As we sat down, the congregants were still singing the same song "Trust in the Lord and don't despair, He is a friend so true." I later learned that this was the only song that this new congregation had learned, thus the repetition. When it was time for the sermon, I looked up and to my surprise, standing behind the pulpit was "the caretaker!" Now it all began to make sense; this was why my mother had looked so concerned when he and his friend were there earlier in the day. He was, in fact, the preacher of this new little church in Lenasia.

This pastor had quite a few sisters, and a friendly group of young people in his church. The pastor called up his sisters to sing and they harmonized so beautifully. They extended a warm welcome to me, and quickly became my friends in this new environment for all of us. One afternoon the young pastor came to visit our home. He wrote a note asking me if he could speak to me in private. He then asked my brother Thachie if he would bring me by his place to visit. I wondered if I had done something wrong. The church had so many rules, and I thought that I may have broken one. I was pleasantly surprised to learn that the young handsome pastor was in fact interested in me. My mom soon discovered his interest, when he brought over flowers and sometimes chocolate, to the delight of my little sister Sylvie. I soon married the charming young preacher when I was almost seventeen. Although I was a young bride then, I am happy to say that I am still married to that same preacher 56 years later! I am so thankful for the wonderful blessings we have had over these many years together, particularly the blessing of a large family.

Today, Sam often jokes that in the USA, people ask why we have such a large family, while in South Africa, people wondered why we had such a small family. He responds that when we were first married, we planned to have a girl and a boy. The first was a girl and so were the second, third and fourth. The fifth was a boy. We then went into the second stage of family planning, and planned to have another boy so that our son Neil could have a brother as well. The sixth child arrived, also a girl! Thus we advise young couples, not to spend time in family planning, but to just take the first two children that arrive! Though we joke this way, we truly believe that each of our six children, has a special purpose. It pleases us that they have faith and strongly believe in giving to others, as they have been beneficiaries of countless blessings.

I look back and am amazed by the provision of God in the most difficult circumstances. He definitely had his hand on us and carried us through. My prayer is that my children will continue to place their reliance on God.

After fifty six years of marriage, now with six children, 3 sons-in-law, a daughter-in-law, and five grandchildren, this preacher, "my caretaker," is still taking great care of me.

Samuel and Sue wed, February 10, 1962

9

THE YOUNG PREACHER

by Samuel Moonsamy

As a young teenager, I wanted to know who God was, and where God was. I remember lying in bed one day and thinking about God. In my frustration, I prayed a simple prayer, "God, I do not know who you are, or where you are, but please just reveal yourself to me."

About 3 months later, missionaries settled in our area, and built a church in the neighborhood. As young kids, we enjoyed playing around the building. Being raised in the slums and being the rough kids that we were, for fun we would often play in the long grass next to the church and throw rocks onto the church roof. At times in the evenings, the rocks would hit or break a window. When the attendees would come out of the church to see what had happened, holding lamps in their hands, we would lay in the long grass, trying to hold in our laughter. At that time, we thought we were having fun.

Around Christmas time, a young boy from the same church came to invite kids to attend their Christmas program. We picked a fight with him, and he was not such a great Christian after all. He raised his fists to fight back. We tackled him, rolling around in the red South African sand. He broke loose and we chased him as he ran toward the church and narrowly escaped into a side door. My friend Gwayne and I stood there anxiously waiting for him to come out. Before we knew it, the door flung open. A stern woman peered down at us and wanted to know what we wanted, and if we wanted to come in. Before we could answer any of her questions, she got a hold of me by the scruff of my neck (my shirt collar), and literally flung me into the church. My friend Gwayne who was a lot thinner than me, flew past me. We gathered ourselves together and got seated at the front row of the church. This was our first introduction to the Christian church!

The people in the church were very nice to us, and invited us to come back again for service on Sunday. We obliged and attended the service thinking we would be doing them a favor for their kindness toward us that day. When they stood up, we stood up, when they sang, we mumbled and pretended to know what we were doing. When they read, we listened. Then it was time for the message. The minister opened his Bible and read from John Chapter 3, Verse 16. To our young South African ears it was difficult to understand an American accent. Americans say we have accents. We think that Americans have accents. What made it even worse was that he was from the state of Texas. Thankfully his message was simple enough to grasp and I prayed a simple prayer of faith.

The Texan, Rev Poteet and a local minister, Rev Taylor were two amazing mentors in my life. My family was devastated though, when they found out that I was following "the white man's God," as they called it.

I went home and could not openly talk about my new experience. However, when my family eventually found out, they were very unhappy. I always tell American kids, that way back there in Africa, we had a great respect for the American flag. They ask why, and I tell them, my mother, she gave us the stripes, and we saw the stars. When my mom found out, I saw more stars than I had ever seen in my lifetime. My father called a family meeting and asked me to stand in the presence of his brothers and sisters. He demanded that I denounce the "white man's God" and break ties with my new friends. As a young boy, I had never ever spoken back to my father, but that day I told him quietly that I was sorry, but I was not prepared to do so. My father was very angry with me. He slammed his fist on the table, pointed his finger at me and said "I want you to know, that you are not a part of this family anymore."

While my family did not kick me out of the house, at the young age of 15, I could feel and knew that there was a clear separation between them and me. This was very difficult as I loved my family dearly. I remained in my home as my parents thought that I was too young to be totally abandoned. I quietly studied the scriptures, while alone. Within one week, I read the gospels of Matthew, Mark, Luke, and John, and went back to the church to ask for a bible. My mentors counseled me and said "you have been reading the bible." I replied, "but the bible is spelled B-I-B-L-E not Matthew, Mark, Luke and John." They laughed and opened the bible to show me that these books were in the bible. I did not realize that I was already reading the bible. They found an old tattered bible for me. I would say I read it cover to cover....but it was so tattered and torn, there were no covers.

A few years later, I felt that I was being called to the ministry. I remained in my home and showed the utmost respect to my family. Eventually the bonds between us were mended and by now my family was very accepting and positive toward me. Many even joined me. I attended Bible College and thus continued my new journey of faith.

10

COME UNTO ME ALL YE THAT LABOR AND ARE HEAVY LADEN

told by Sue Moonsamy
written by her daughter Priscilla Moonsamy

I T was 1976, a politically turbulent year in South Africa. My sister Sylvie and I were cutting meat, cleaning, and setting up for the customers that would visit my new butcher shop. Through a string of miracles, I had bought the business a few months prior. The business was located directly across from the bustling Oriental Plaza (so named as it was an all Indian shopping complex) on Main Street in Fordsburg, and people would stop by on their way home from work, to get some meat for dinner. The days were busy as we developed the tools for this new trade and we did our best to serve the ebb and flow of customers.

One day surely stands out as an extraordinary day. A young woman came rushing into the store in a panic. My sister Sylvie rushed to her side and noticed that she was very pregnant, and going into labor. She needed an ambulance to rush her to the nearest hospital; actually, the nearest black hospital, which was far away. We rushed to the telephone and called the hospital. The hospital assured us that an ambulance would be on its way. From experience, however, we knew that we could not depend on an ambulance to get to any scene very quickly in South Africa, for a person of color. Before we could even ask her for any details, the woman slumped down onto the floor of the store and was writhing in pain. John, our strong muscular employee who was never afraid of anything, ran out of the store shaking, and closed the door behind him. We immediately sprang into action. We locked the business door, grabbed some newspapers and started to cover up the glass windows, as a very curious crowd started gathering outside the store wondering what was happening. We comforted the expectant mom and tried to help her in whatever way we could. Though not medically qualified to help, both Sylvie and I had given birth to 6 kids each, and knew the process of labor very well. Sylvie coached this young mother as she gave birth to a beautiful little baby girl, right on the floor of the butcher store.

A doctor that was passing by heard the commotion and came in to help cut the cord, after the birth of this precious new baby. As the sound of the siren of the ambulance neared, Sylvie struggled to contain her emotion. It seemed like a whole day had just passed, though it had been just a couple of hours. Of course it took the ambulance over an hour to arrive at the scene. By the time the ambulance arrived, the young new mother lay silent, relieved that the little baby that she was cradling, seemed to be doing well. As the ambulance, loaded with mom and baby, rushed off to the hospital, Sylvie and I hugged each other and cried as reality set in. We had just helped bring a new life into this world.

After a few days, the lady returned to the store with her beautiful baby girl. She thanked us sincerely holding both her hands together in genuine African appreciation as she relayed her story to us. She was walking on Main street when she suddenly started to feel contractions. She did not think that they were real and continued on her way to try and make it to the bus stop so she could get home. As she walked on, the contractions strengthened in duration and severity. In fear and all alone, she walked into a store to ask if someone there would help her by calling an ambulance, but the storekeeper refused. "I knew you would help me when I saw your poster" she said, pointing to the poster on our store window. The verse on the poster read, *"Come unto me all ye that labor and are heavy laden and I will give you rest"* (Matthew 11:28). We did not think that the caption on the poster would be taken so literally! Word got around and a few days later this story was covered in The Star, a Johannesburg newspaper, with a picture of Sylvie and myself next to the poster. The local Lenasia Times newspaper, in the neighborhood where we lived, also ran the story.

We are truly thankful to God that this beautiful baby arrived safely into the world, though in a very difficult situation. The mom named the baby "Sylvie" after my sister. This young mom was from the homelands (barren lands set aside for certain black groups under the system of Apartheid) and was not allowed within most of South Africa legally, even though her family had probably been in the country for many generations, likely even before the white settlers had arrived.

Unfortunately, baby Sylvie was born into the stark reality of Apartheid, but we pray that God has used her life in a profound and meaningful way. We lost touch with mom and baby, who likely returned to the homeland. We hope that someday we will have the opportunity to meet this young lady again and personally relate the incredible miracle of her arrival.

11

A Surprise Grocery Delivery

told by Samuel Moonsamy
written by his daughter Priscilla Moonsamy

O N this particular, cold winter morning, frost covered the ground, as I drove Sue to the train station in the town of Lenasia, so she could take the early morning train to the city where she had recently found a job. It was challenging to raise our children with the little salary I earned from the church, so Sue was really glad when she was hired by a company to wire computer plaques to be used for programming. I thank God for Sue who was always such a hardworking mom and pastor's wife, truly dedicated to God, her family, and to the church family.

As I drove back home, I stopped at the railway crossing

to make sure that there were no trains coming. I was always careful at the crossing since we had seen a number of fatal car and train collisions. Our family had resided in a parsonage, across from the railway line for many years. Our home was located just about a mile away from the train station itself, a very busy train station in Lenasia, a township set aside in 1956, for people of Indian origin.

Now that there were about 100,000 residents in a rapidly growing community, less than 20 years later, it was hard to believe that both Sue and I were a part of the first fifty families, that were moved into this area, when the Group Areas Act became law. We had gradually grown to love Lenasia because both of our families were here, and we made friends who became like family to us. This area held a lot of important history for us as we developed the first church here. My dear friend, Pastor Gwayne Challen, and I had previously held church meetings in tents in various locations. We rode on our bicycles to those sites to conduct church services there.

On the other side of the railway line was a military camp. This is where we all lived when we were initially forcibly moved into the area, into military style barracks, that each family cordoned off with curtains or furniture. Outhouses (communal toilets) were available for restrooms, with faucets (taps) outside that provided the families with running water.

Now, as we moved to the other side of the tracks, we looked across the railway line but did not really know what kinds of operations were being carried out in this military site. We would see soldiers training and we knew that there was an ammunition factory there since Sue's mom had worked there. While she worked there, Sue's mom just carried out her duties and did what she was told. She died when she was still pretty young and we wondered if the work she had done could have contributed to a shortened life, since both her mom and grandmother had lived to be over a 100 years old. In South Africa at the time, questions like these could not be asked.

In our home, we would awaken early in the morning to the sounds of beautiful African voices as workers sang while they carried heavy equipment as they worked near the railway lines. Their voices permeated the air in smooth, amazing harmony. The young white supervisors standing nearby directed the workflow of the day. It was truly unbelievable that the most beautiful music was made during hard labor and daily struggle. Fortunately the white supervisors could not understand the language of the songs for a hopeful future. The music foretold that someday South Africa would be a free country, with everyone treated as equals.

After I dropped Sue at the station so that she could take the train to work, as I drove away, I rolled down my window to listen to the strong voices of hope. As I looked toward the men who labored and sang in unison, I noticed some kids nearby the railway tracks throwing rocks (stones) at something. I pulled the car over to the side of the road and tried to walk down toward the railway tracks. The terrain was a bit rough and steep and I lost my balance a couple of times but managed to stay on my feet. I called out to the kids to find out what they were doing so close to the tracks. I was concerned that a train may be swiftly passing by soon and that these young kids may be in danger. As I got closer, I noticed that they were throwing rocks at a grocery bag lying nearby the train tracks. I started running as I got closer to them and they told me that they thought that there was a cat or an animal in the bag since they could hear sounds coming from the bag. I asked them to stop throwing stones and to move further out so that they would not be too close to the railway tracks. I ran over to see what was in the bag and to my utter surprise, I saw a tiny little newborn infant probably just born a very short while ago, nestled in the grocery bag, on a blanket, the placenta and umbilical cord still intact. I grabbed the baby and looked around to see if I could spot the mother or someone nearby.

As I stood there with the baby in my arms, I thought about baby Moses and how he was left in a basket on the river, while his sister watched him float. I wondered if this little one's mom was wondering if he had been found, if he was still alive, if he would be better off dead in this country where life would be so difficult for anyone with darker skin. I thought about the mom and knew that she was probably considered illegal in the country of her birth. She was likely unable to receive any medical attention from the clinics or hospitals nearby since she had probably crossed a border a few miles away to work and earn some money to send home to her family. Had she tried to get medical attention in South Africa, she may have been imprisoned, or deported to her homeland where conditions were even worse. How old was she? Did she have any other family members or other kids?

As these questions flooded my mind, I thought about the midwives I knew in Lenasia, amazing pioneers in our community. If only the mom of this precious newborn had known of them, she may have had a different story. Below is an excerpt of my recent write-up online, to honor these amazing women and to remind the younger generation of our heroes:

> *The Mother Teresa's of Lenasia who may have delivered you. They made history with hard work, sweat, and tears. C.O.D. (Cash on Delivery), also FREE if you did not have money. In the fifties, when Indians were moved*

to the two Lenz Military Camps, there were three ladies whom I knew: Paul Partie, Auntie Ella David, and Mrs. Susan Fredericks and I have heard a few others too, who walked from patient to patient in the Camps and the growing township under great difficulty, with little or no transportation to deliver some of you. Mrs. Fredericks lived at Protea and travelled on a scooter. They did everything from prenatal care to postnatal care. Delivery was the most important part of their work, after often staying up for nights. Then they took care of the patient and baby for TEN DAYS, washing the napkins (diapers) and when all was done they received their payment of TEN RANDS. Can you believe that you may have been a Ten Rand baby! Then, there were no hospitals within the township.

An elderly lady, who had also noticed the commotion down below, jolted my mind back to the time at the railway tracks, as she tried to climb down the hill. As I left the area and got closer to her, she helped to console the crying baby. When we got to the car, we tried to make the baby comfortable by wrapping this little one in a scarf. We noticed that it was a teeny little boy likely just about a couple of hours old. The lady offered to carry the baby on her lap while I drove to the nearest clinic. We did not have seatbelt laws and car seats then. The doctors checked the baby and after a while found that he was in good health. The clinic staff nicknamed him Samuel, which is my given name.

I called Sue at work briefly, and when she got home, she

and I talked seriously about adopting this baby. Though by this time we already had five children of our own, we knew that God would take care of us, as He always had done, through all of the tough times. We were willing to do what we could, to give this little baby boy a home. The doctors directed me to the Social Welfare office which was a tiny little room with not much to offer, to request registration documents and procedures for adopting the baby. The social welfare office took the baby and told me what I had feared, that we were not allowed to adopt him since he was a Black African baby. I argued that we were African too, though of Indian origin. At the time that the baby was found, the four race groups had been clearly defined in South Africa and each race group was designated or assigned to specific areas of living and schooling. I protested profusely, but to no avail. I had to leave and received no further communication regarding baby "Samuel." I called the office several times and was told that the baby was being taken care of and would either be sent to an orphanage or be placed in adoption services.

To this day, I wonder what has happened to that little baby. He would now be over 40 years old. Could he be a teacher, a lawyer, a doctor, a social worker? Is he still alive? Where is he living? Did he ever find a family that would love and care for him? As our family huddled around our coal stove, that cold winter night, we thanked God that baby Samuel was saved that day. We said a prayer for him and had to let him go, but baby Samuel has always remained in our hearts.

12

Ja Meneer, Kan Ek U Help? (Yes Sir, Can I Help You?)

by Samuel Moonsamy

I
T was not customary for South Africans in general to address a person of color as "Sir" or "Madam" because as non-whites, we were always considered of lower class. In the early days even the newspapers would refer to blacks by their first names, and whites as "Mr." or "Mrs."

During this time in South Africa, very rarely would people of color be called by any title normally used for whites. We were used to the brusque mannerisms of the privileged classes. "Ja, wat soek jy?" "Yes what do you want?" Sometimes they would add the not so nice, unceremonious addendum, "boy." Typically most Afrikaners (South Africans of Dutch origin) in the presence of other Afrikaners would avoid addressing anyone of color in a conventionally respectful manner. This was strictly reserved for whites.

Afrikaans Medium

I had a knack for learning Afrikaans. At times I considered it my first language and learned to master most of the idioms and manners of speech. Early in life I learned the character and genius of the language and was able to converse freely in a formal or colloquial way. This was due, by and large, to my early education in Afrikaans medium schools and because the friends we associated with were mostly Afrikaans speaking "Coloureds," Blacks and Indians.

Communication at Work

Years later, while working as a bookkeeper for a business known as Flower Centre, I was, at times, required to talk to the clients. One company in particular, the South African Railways, was very important because it collected the Cash on Deliveries (COD's) from customers in Cape Town, Bloemfontein, and Durban. On a monthly basis they distributed the checks for the amounts they had collected. Because these amounts sometimes ran into thousands, part of my job was to inquire about the payments by telephone.

Knowing that the people at the financial offices of the Railways generally spoke Afrikaans, I engaged them in hearty conversation. Because I was able to converse in their language, they addressed me on the telephone as "Meneer," the equivalent of "Sir" in English. The conversation would normally go like this:

"Hullo Meneer Van der Merwe, hoe gaan dit vanmore?"

"Ja nee Meneer Samuel, dit gaan nog baie goed."

"En hoe gaan dit nog met u?"

"Met my gaan dit nog heeltemaal goed."

"Sê vir my meneer, is die tjek nou gereed?"

"Ja seker, Meneer. Wanneer wil u dit optel?"

Translation:

Hello Mr. Van der Merwe how are you this morning?

Oh yes Mr. Samuel, it's going very well with me. How are you?

(Mr. Samuel was the name by which they knew me)

With me, everything is still very well too.

Tell me Sir, is the check ready for pickup?

Yes Sir, it's definitely ready. When do you want to send for it?

Usually we would send a messenger to pick up the check. After having developed a kind of friendship over the telephone with the manager for over a year, I decided that I would personally collect the check because we did not have a messenger present that day.

I parked the car at the back of the Johannesburg train station, also known as Park Station, and walked briskly up the stairs to the required floor where I presented myself at the front desk. "Ja, wat soek jy?" "Yes, what do you want?" was the curt question from the young lady on the other side. I replied in Afrikaans that I would like to see the manager. She immediately asked if I had an appointment. I affirmed that I had personally spoken to the manager and he had told me to ask for him.

She went to the back of the partition and told them that a person by the name of Samuel was there to talk to the manager. He came to the counter and I told him that my name was Samuel at which he was taken aback. "Wat!" (What!) he shouted, "Is jy die Meneer Samuels, met wie ek nou net gepraat het op die foon?" (Are you the Mister Samuels that I just spoke to on the phone?) "Presies meneer." (Exactly Sir), I replied.

At this he ran back and whispered to the other co-workers, "Jong kom kyk julle, hier is die "tjara" Meneer wat altyd bel!" (Oh my goodness, come look, this is Mister Coolie that always calls!) They came to the front and all of them looked at me, then looked at each other, and began laughing. They were laughing at him for unwittingly calling me "Sir" all this time in Afrikaans. He was under the impression because of my fluent Afrikaans, that I was a white Afrikaner.

What made it more convincing was that I also spoke with a strong expressive Afrikaans accent. In most cases when people of color did speak the language they faltered with the accent which immediately allowed Afrikaaners to detect that they were in fact non-white.

He gave me the check and then looked at me in a friendly manner saying: "Jong ou Sam, sê vir my waar het jy so blerrie lekker Afrikaans geleer?" (Tell me Sam, where did you learn to speak Afrikaans so bloody well?)

What he did not know was that there were many Indians who could speak Afrikaans meticulously because of the schools we attended and also because of the friends we had, particularly those living in country towns where Afrikaans was the dominant language.

Background in Languages

Like many others I attended Afrikaans medium schools at Evaton and later at Kliptown and read many Afrikaans books, most importantly, I read my Afrikaans Bible. While many people did not care much for Afrikaans, I read South African newspapers daily, particularly the Transvaler and the Daily

Mail and by doing this, I learned to master the language.

My Mother's Tongues

My mother, who never went to school, learned to speak English, Afrikaans, Zulu and Tamil. It is interesting that, though she was considered uneducated or illiterate, she always had a great respect for education. She encouraged her children against so many odds to learn the languages of all the people with whom we lived, and to excel at school.

The Advantages of Knowing a Language

Despite the pressure of the Afrikaner people as an undermining political force, knowing the language actually put us in an advantageous position. We always knew what the Afrikaner was saying about us. As kids we played with them at the "vlei" (marshes) making "klei osse and waens" (clay oxen and wagons). We knew how to swing a "klei lat" (Stick with wet clay at the end which we swung at each other in make-belief war). Sometimes a few of them would come together, and say "Kom ons bliksem die tjaras" (Come let's beat up the Coolies). Knowing what they were planning, we prepared ourselves for attack or got out of their way quickly before they could strike. Those Indians who did not know what they were saying, fell foul to their devious ways.

South African Blacks usually spoke the language of the oppressor as well as one or more languages, such as Zulu, Sotho or Xhosa. The government could have been oblivious to any plans for insurrection, because of the lack of understanding of the local languages. The disenfranchised people, on the other hand, have always understood the language of the "master."

This indeed put us in a far more advantageous position than the oppressor who, in most cases, did not bother to learn the languages of the people. Though admittedly there also are some Afrikaners and other white folk who did embrace and learn the languages of the country. However, some spoke a pidgin Zulu known as "Fanagalo," a demeaning slang of the Zulu language belittling the people who were very proud of their language and culture, and had maintained and preserved their proud culture and history as the original owners of the land.

Not all Afrikaners were brutal and oppressive. Many individuals, like the friends we developed while working with Campus Crusade for Christ, who always welcomed us to their homes and taught their children to call us "Oom en Tannie" (Uncle and Aunt). According to South African culture, this was the proper way for a child, any child, to address any adult. It was considered highly disrespectful if they called any adult on their first name. It was very difficult for our kids to address anyone older by their first names on our arrival to the USA, but some people preferred to not be called uncle or aunt, or Mr or Mrs, so our kids eventually adjusted.

Some Afrikaans friends treated us well and always felt very uncomfortable about the treatment meted out to us by the government, and they condemned the government as unchristian in their laws against us.

Some of the Afrikaans kids were caught in this trap unknowingly thinking that what they were doing was just natural and normal as the system and some of their parents had taught them. I heard about two little white Afrikaner children who were sent to the corner Indian store to buy sugar. The boy addressed the shopkeeper in this manner: "Koelie, my ma vra asseblief een pond suiker?" (Coolie, my mom would like a pound of sugar please?) His sister, realizing that he had crossed the line by addressing the man in a derogatory manner, shouted at him. "Het jy nie maniere nie? Kan jy nie sé Oom Koelie nie?" (Don't you have manners? Can you not say Uncle Coolie?) Koelie, pronounced and spelled in English as Coolie, is a derogatory word for Indians. These poor kids had to be pitied for their naivete. In this case it was evident that this was the normal way to refer to Indians in their homes.

Today we meet many Afrikaners who have emigrated to the U.S. They are usually very happy to meet us and also to converse with us in Afrikaans. Now their kids address me as Oom (Uncle) and my wife as Tante (Aunt) or Meneer en Mevrou (Mr and Mrs). We reciprocate with compassion, understanding and appreciation, but it makes us think of how this was not the normal exchange at that time in South Africa, sadly.

Recently, while my wife and I visited New Zealand and Australia, we met several South Africans with whom we had friendly communication in Afrikaans. Many Afrikaners excitedly welcomed us and talked to us addressing us as "Sir and Ma'am" in Afrikaans. I cannot help but wonder if the man at the Railway Station Offices did not also move to New Zealand or Australia or even to the United States, and maybe he or his children now would refer to us as "Meneer en Mevrou." It is just not so funny anymore.

13

My Business Endeavor

told by Sue Moonsamy
written by her daughter Noelene Moonsamy

I never dreamed that one day I would be the proud owner of a meat market, or butcher shop, as we called it in South Africa.

I was selling calendars for Boystown, an American company raising money for a boys school in South Africa (a white boys' school, as I later learned!). I walked into a butcher shop in Fordsburg on Main street across from the Oriental Plaza (close to Johannesburg). The butcher owner, an Indian lady, ordered a calendar from me and asked me if I would be interested in helping her with her business. She owned a restaurant (take-away/takeout eatery) next door and needed help. Though I had no prior experience in this industry, in need of more income with a family to care for, I eagerly accepted the position

91

as manager of the butcher shop. About a month later, she decided to put the butcher shop on the market for sale. Since I had quickly learned how to manage the shop, I told the owner that I was interested in purchasing it, a crazy idea, since I had no money! The business owner wanted R5000. Interestingly, unlike today, the rand was actually stronger in value than the US dollar during this time, likely due to South Africa's rich natural resources such as gold, diamonds and many other minerals. My husband was working as a pastor with very little income. To care for his family with six kids, he supplemented his income by doing the accounting for a Flower Market at the time. He took a loan as an advance from his company, in exchange for a few months of work without pay, obviously a huge risk!

Non-white people were not allowed to own businesses in that area, so the business was licensed to a white man.

My sister Sylvie helped me in the business, where we both worked tirelessly. My husband Sam helped with the bookkeeping when it was possible. The only other employee we had was John, who had been hired by the previous owner. He became a part of our family. John was a man who came from Soweto, a neighboring township. He was a strong man who had a heart of gold. John could cut meat, with the large corporate cutters, better than any other meat cutter. He was also a great help when it came to lifting the huge beef or lamb carcasses that would hang from hooks in the large walk-in freezer. John would help us as we sliced, minced, filled, tenderized, and processed the meat until it was packaged and ready for sale.

When we first opened the business, our entire livelihood depended on its income, since Sam was working on his advance now with no income from his current job. We were strapped for cash, when a woman came in asking for bones to make soup for her kids, since she could not afford meat. She had 50 cents in her pocket and the bones sold for R1.00. When I told her the price, her expression changed and she walked sadly to the door. My mind flashed back to the time when my siblings and I sat at our dinner table with very little to eat. I imagined this lady going back to her kids not having anything to feed them. "Wait," I called out to her and packed the bones, then added steak, eggs, and butter. She looked at me confused and said 'I only have 50 cents.' I told her "Don't worry about the money" and gave her the food that I had packed for her family. She was overwhelmed with thankfulness. Little did we realize that she worked at the huge Adonis factory. When she returned to her job, she told all of her co-workers about her experience.

From that moment on, the business became so busy with factory laborers, that we could barely keep up with the demand. On Fridays, the queue (line) curved out of the door for our Boerewors, a South African sausage, similar to Bratwurst, but with its own unique spices and flavor. I added a special Indian secret spice combination to the original spice that seemed to make the flavor burst out of the casings. Boerewors, along with other meats, grace the grills of almost every braai (BBQ), along with pap (corn-meal), hot spicy tomato chutney, and other sides with mouth-watering flavors of which South Africans are so proud. Hospitality is so ingrained in the society, that even the poorest of the poor would share whatever they have.

Sylvie, John, and I worked long and hard in that butcher shop. We came to know the neighbors and felt really comfortable there. My kids loved visiting on Saturdays. They would reach their little hands into the cash register, grab some coins and run to the store next door, to buy sweets (candy). The Mono Bakery at the corner had amazing pink and white meringue cookies, baked to perfection with mainly sugar and egg-whites. Though not nutritious, the kids thought that it was the best dessert ever!

One day John, who hardly ever missed a day at work, did not feel well so he took a day off. The business was open and bustling as usual. We had a large order of beef to fill for the next day and, without John, I was concerned that we would not have it ready in time. Sylvie and I decided to try to cut all of the meat ourselves. We walked into the large refrigerator and I tried to unhook half a beef carcass. It was just too heavy to carry alone. We tried to lift it together and managed to get the meat off the hook. It was massive and much heavier than it looked. Since our arms could not hold the weight, the carcass fell swiftly to the ground trapping both of us under it. To our horror, the door to the freezer had slammed shut, locking us inside. Sam had just left the business to run some errands, and was not going to return till the end of the day. We could freeze to death! Was this the end of our lives? Sylvie and I struggled and tried to free ourselves, but could not move an inch. We started shivering and shaking with cold and fear. We lay there praying and hoping someone would find us. We called and screamed and shouted but to no avail.

We were about to give up when we heard a noise. Sam had returned to retrieve something that he had accidentally left behind. We screamed for help and he heard our cries, opened the freezer doors and managed to help us out. God answered our prayers that day!

The butcher shop was located in Fordsburg, not far from the large metropolitan city of Johannesburg. It was a bright little store that we kept clean and neat with much pride. This was the first time I started to tap into the entrepreneurial skill that I did not realize I possessed. Even though I was never very close to my father's family, as my parents were separated at an early age, I knew that his family was very successful in business. Though my parents had separated and my mom was left to raise five kids with very little money, I probably had some of my dad's business acumen in my genes, though I had no formal training. My butcher shop was located in a busy business district. In the evenings we would look across the street to see buses lined up heading out to the different neighborhoods - Soweto for Blacks, Eldorado Park for Coloureds, and Lenasia for Indians. Non-whites were not allowed to stay in the city overnight so everyone was streaming home to their respective neighborhoods.

Main Street was a very busy street with not many robots (signal lights) or crosswalks for pedestrians, and people would often get hit by vehicles, as they ran across. On one occasion, one of our friends walked across the street toward our store. As she got closer to the business and waved to us, a car came by and hit her! We were in a shocked state! We watched as her body took the impact, flew up high and landed on the ground. We rushed her off to the hospital praying and hoping for a miracle. Miraculously, not a single bone was broken, despite the fact that the car that had hit her looked like it had been crushed. We often teased her that she was stronger than that vehicle. It was such a relief to see her healthy and well with no injuries. We saw many miracles in those days, even humor was a miraculous gift of comfort that kept our minds sane.

Early one morning, at the crack of dawn, before the sun shone on the red sand of the African horizon, a man walked into the store. John's bus had not yet arrived and Sylvie and I were alone in the store setting up for the day. His face was covered by his cap and he was dressed in all black. He reached forward for the eggs in an attempt to steal. I realized what was going on and walked toward him as he held a stern and steady gaze. Sylvie froze in place. I was terrified at that moment, and I was angry. I had no idea how dangerous this man was. I wondered if I was going to lose my life. I had poured sweat and tears into this endeavor and I had grown to love my business! A still voice in my head said, "You say repay evil with evil, but I will repay evil with good." I gathered up whatever strength I could at that moment and said, "Sir, please do not hurt us," as I reached for the eggs his hand was on, picked it up, and placed it in his hand. "Take this, it is for you." He hesitated, then turned toward me. His hard gaze softened. Embarrassed, he took the eggs and walked out. As he turned, I noticed a large blade in his back pocket and thanked God for sparing our lives that day. I later found out that he was a known gang member in the neighborhood at the time. I never called the cops. On another occasion, I called the ambulance for him when he came in bloody after being stabbed, and comforted and talked with him while he lay in pain waiting for help.

We noticed a change in him toward us. He would stop by and check on us frequently, making sure we were okay. One day the police came by looking for him. I watched sadly as they pushed him into a police van for a crime about which I preferred not to know. I knew God had the power to change him and had seen this change in his life already. I can only hope that he was able to make that transition.

We owned the butcher for three years and it more than supplemented Sam's full time pastor's salary of R35/month. For the first time, we were able to provide the necessities for our family, John's family, and Sylvie's family that we could not afford previously. Because of the situation in South Africa, we sadly lost this business which was our only viable source of income, when the white licensed owner suddenly sold it without any remuneration to us. I had no legal ownership of the store and could not even dispute the issue. In an instant, I lost everything for which I had worked so hard. Though I realized that my experience and newfound knowledge could never be taken away, I still cried bitter tears.

Almost 20 years later, my smile turned into a beam of pride when my daughter asked if I would manage her new practice, after her graduation from the School of Optometry, at UC Berkeley.

Painting by Alisha Moonsamy Abrahams

14

BLANKE FAMILIE IN 'N ONGELUK BETROKKE (WHITE FAMILY IN AN ACCIDENT)

by Samuel Moonsamy

I T was late on a Sunday afternoon at our home in Lenasia, when we were sitting around talking about the happenings of the day. The six children were either busy playing or getting ready to do their homework for Monday. Outside, a car stopped. This was not uncommon as our smaller road ran parallel to the main road across an open strip of land bordered by a railroad. It was not unusual for family or friends to stop by unannounced. It was a bit unusual, though, to see a white person. The nearest white area would be in the city about twenty miles away.

As usual, we peered through the opening of the curtains on the front windows and saw the familiar face of Mrs. Bertha McDelling, accompanied by her three daughters. They got out of the car. The white driver waved and sped off.

From her, we learned that while traveling on the Roodepoort Road, intersecting the Old Potchefstroom highway at the four-way stop, they met with an accident. The black man who had hit them from behind was unconscious but all of them in the McDelling car had escaped, unhurt. Their car, she told us, had a huge dent where the other car had ploughed into them.

A passing white motorist stopped to give them assistance. They accepted and gave him directions to our home, roughly three miles from the site of the accident. Fortunately we were nearby and he was happy to oblige, apparently thinking they were white. Mrs. McDelling was as white as any other white person in South Africa. Her hair was blond, just as the hair of her three daughters, and she could easily be mistaken for white. Their family came from Cape Town, where typically many who looked white because of mixed heritage, were declared "Coloured."

By the time I arrived at the scene of the accident, the black man was already removed from the car and laid on a grassy area away from moving traffic. The front of his car, a Volkswagen, was severely dented. The person who stopped to give them a ride also promised to call the police and ambulance from his house for we were not yet in the cell phone era. Before I left home I also called the emergency number reporting the accident and was assured that an ambulance would be on the way.

After my arrival at the scene of the accident, a police car stopped asking if the man was dead. "No sir," we replied, he's

still breathing and alive." The policemen in the next four police cars that stopped, all asked the same question: "Waar is
die blanke familie in die ongeluk betrokke?" (Where is the
white family that was involved in an accident?). We informed
them that it was not a white family but a "kleurling familie" or
"Coloured family." They assured us that the black ambulance
would be coming as they had already radioed for them. They
then sped off hastily.

We stood around the black man discussing the immediate
emergency of a man who needed medical attention and the
length of time it was taking for the ambulance to come. All the
while we could hear the occasional rushing of a speeding car
on the highway. Intermittently a police car would stop with the
policeman asking the same question, yet again. Obviously, the
concern was only for the "blanke familie," the "white family."

About two hours later the non-white ambulance, from the
non-white hospital of Leratong or Baragwanath, clearly identi-
fiable as non-white by a green stripe painted around its white
body, finally made its presence. It came chugging along and
came to a stop, before almost knocking us over. Two men, the
driver and the assistant, got out and made their way through
the grass to us."What's wrong with this man?" they asked. "He
drink too much Itchwala (beer) hey," they laughed. By the smell
of their breath and their inability to stand erect, we sensed
that they in fact had drunk too much itchwala, and were both
quite inebriated.

This, however, did not deter them from lifting the man
onto the gurney/stretcher. As they lifted him, one of them let
go of the one side and the man fell off onto the ground. With
our help they finally loaded their patient into the ambulance
and drove off into the distance, heading for Baragwanath Hospital another 13 miles away. The next day Pastor McDelling

found the patient sitting up in his bed fully recovered and none the worse for the experience. We were concerned, but fortunately he had survived the whole ordeal. The patient offered to pay for the damage to the other vehicle and asked that the matter be kept private as he was under the influence also, and should not have driven in that condition.

This incident was a strange one with a representation of all of South Africa's major race groups, White, Black, "Coloured" and Indian.

All four of these representatives of the racially segregated South Africa, victims of a skewed system that deluded and defined people according to their skin color and cultural heritage, were in a cruel and vicious drama of race, played on the stage of a world of prejudice, bigotry and racial inequity. They were all children of South Africa, unwittingly acting out a drama for which they were not responsible.

At the time of this story, the McDellings with their family lived at Promosa, Potchefstroom (the "Coloured" area), roughly seventy miles away from where we lived. Our ways parted as I moved on to another organization. Once, after we moved to the states, we met at Cape Town and they indicated that they too wanted to move somewhere where they would have freedom to live as normal human beings.

It is, however, never easy to move to another country when you consider the difficulties involved. Uprooting yourself from one country to another and starting all over again is an enormous task and extremely difficult. We told them that we would be praying for them.

We later learned that the McDelling family had indeed moved to London. They told us that their son went on a visit to England and while there discovered that because Bertha's dad was a British subject, that by virtue of her relationship to him, she had a right to settle in England with her family. We had the pleasure of reconnecting in London in 2017. Together we sat down for dinner at a hotel near the airport and reminisced about this story.

During our visit in London, I chided and teased George, telling him that the government in South Africa was looking for him. Keen to know why, I told him, "because you violated 'The prohibition of Mixed Marriages Act,' also known as the "Immorality Act." Sue and I rejoiced with them for having had a successful marriage for so many years and also that they raised a wonderful family in both South Africa and England.

Galations 3:28 *There is neither Jew nor Greek, there is neither slave nor free, there is neither male nor female; for you are all one in Christ Jesus.*

.

15

ELECTION DAY

by Melanie Moonsamy
daughter of Samuel and Sue Moonsamy

I N 1984 so-called Indians and "Coloureds" were invited to the polls. What the government hailed and presented to the world as a big step toward Democracy, was scoffed at by people of color and anti-Apartheid supporters, as a major step backward.

Whites, "Coloureds" and Indians would not sit together in the same parliament. Instead the current vein of racial separation and white dominance would run through a segregated government structure. Elected Indians would join the newly formed "House of Delegates" while elected "Coloureds" would join the brand new "House of Representatives." Any policy passed in any of these newly formed units would have to go on to the White "House of Assembly" for final approval or veto.

The overarching reason that this new "Democracy" was so widely rejected though, was that it still was no Democracy as it excluded over 70% of the population - black South Africans! The Apartheid regime had never been able to rationalize why the majority of South Africans had no right to vote and barely any human rights. They had tried to skirt this embarrassment by creating fake solutions, such as the creation of 10 "homelands," where black South Africans supposedly would be free to vote and govern themselves in these "sovereign states." These states were never recognized in the world, as it was quickly realized that the land designated as "homelands" held none of South Africa's coveted minerals and natural resources. Families were torn apart as the government forcefully moved people, based on tribal affiliation, to these dry, arid "homelands." By stripping away their South African citizenships, "homeland citizens" no longer had the right to live and work in South Africa. These "countries" were recognized by South Africa only. The "leaders" paid to govern these homelands were viewed by the people as paid puppets with only self-interest in mind, such as monetary benefit and security for themselves and their families.

The new "Tricameral Government" was yet another attempt to pull the wool over the eyes of the world, and make international investors believe that South Africa was making progress toward Democracy. The majority of Indians and "Coloureds," appalled to be used as pawns in this grand scheme, vehemently protested.

I remember so well how the weeks leading up to the election day were filled with secret meetings to organize a strategic opposition to these fake elections. At our Friday night church youth meeting, we made "Don't Vote" banners and posters. At Sunday afternoon church gatherings, we learned that for every four white elected officials, two "Coloureds" and one "Indian" would be elected. Even if the Indian and "Coloured" Houses banded together to get a law passed, they would be outnumbered by the "White House." "4:2:1" was another anti-election banner we made, to show the futility that this ratio presented. To limit political gatherings, the government quickly passed a silly law that protesters had to stand 5 feet apart. So as not to break this new law, the day before election day, protesters lined the borders of our Indian Township, Lenasia, by standing 5 feet apart in silent, powerful protest. Amongst them stood moms and grandmothers of many who had been imprisoned, exiled and murdered for standing up against the hated system of Apartheid.

Though required by law, a scarce few Indians and "Coloureds" registered to vote. Most people boycotted voter registration to protest these sham elections. So, though the news reported that only 16% of registered voters actually voted, a much lower percentage voted, since so few eligible voters had even bothered to register to vote. The "don't vote" campaign was a sweeping success.

On election day, we went to the polls with our friends to celebrate the low voter turnout, confirming the successful protest. We shared stories of how candidates were giving people bags of groceries to lure them to the polls and watched them drive poor and older people to the polling station to vote. The sky was blue, the sun was warm and freedom songs filled the air in a spirit of solidarity. It was strange to actually feel a sense of victory over a powerful, brutal government. My parents kept us home from school that day and my dad drove us to the demonstrations, across the street from the polling station. At the Civic Center in Lenasia, various groups of navy and white, then green and yellow, then blue and red clad uniformed students arrived from the various public schools, to join the protest. We greeted each other and the mood was festive.

Then, without warning, riot police with face masks formed a line in front of us and we heard the announcement, "You have three minutes to disperse!" Within seconds, police officers ran into the crowd, hitting men, women and children - anyone in their way, with batons. "Get into the car," dad yelled. We got in, just in time, and dad drove off, trying to avoid people, running in front of and alongside the car.

The evening news that night falsely reported that demonstrators, who had refused to heed the 3 minute warning, had started the altercation with the cops.

During the day, we drove by the polling station several times and watched in disbelief as our town turned into an unfamiliar zone of terror. What started with cops wielding batons, continued into a back and forth battle between the angry protesters and cops. Students threw rocks (stones) and the police would respond by spraying the ever increasing crowd with rubber bullets and tear gas. Makeshift emergency clinics were set up in the backs of stores and vans to treat the wounded. Our friend Wayne received treatment in a makeshift clinic. He had leapt in front of a cop who was about to whip a pregnant woman, and was cut on his face. The cut narrowly missed his left eye. I actually married Wayne many years later, and to this day, my sisters tease him for that act of heroism, to get my attention.

That fateful night, dad slowly drove past the polling station several times, to watch. At one point a cop car followed our car as we drove by. It followed us for a while. Dad pretended to be unconcerned, not to alarm us. He eventually pulled up to a store, and the cop car pulled alongside us. "I need to pick up some bread, guys. I'll be back soon. Wait here," dad said loudly as he quickly exited and went inside, not looking at the cops right next to us. We sat there, holding our breaths, as the two big white officers looked at us and smirked. Then they got out and followed our dad into the store. Susheela shrieked in desperation, "Don't let them take daddy, they can take me!" We still tease her and mimic how she blurted that out. Thankfully, the cops came running back to their car and rushed away with their lights flashing. They probably were called to report back to the polling station.

By nightfall, we could barely breathe through the teargas around the Lenasia Civic Center, the largest polling station in our township. Several fires had been started, and the place looked like a war zone. The next monthly edition of the local newspapers, the "Lenasia Times" and "The Indicator," published cover to cover pictures of the wounded as well as the baton wielding cops. We learned that the same scenes were replicated at polling stations across the country.

The Real Deal

The 1994 elections totally contrasted the 1984 elections, though it was just 10 years later. By this time, our family had moved to the United States, and we watched the news and read the newspaper for any trace of news from our beloved South Africa. Early on a Saturday morning in 1990, my mom came rushing into our bedrooms with unbelievable news; Nelson Mandela was to be released, the following day! We jumped out of our beds and watched this news, in disbelief.

The following day, before the sun would rise in the United States, we went to watch this truly epic event with the Farisani family who lived in our neighborhood in El Cerrito, California at the time. Reverend Farisani had himself been released as a political prisoner in South Africa and was brought to the United States by the Red Cross for treatment after his torture in a South African jail. We had read his book and were honored for the opportunity to get to know him, his wife Regina and their three beautiful children. He invited our family along with other South Africans to watch this historic event, the release of Nelson Mandela, the world's most known political prisoner. News stations had asked to televise our reaction and we saw ourselves on the news that evening, laughing and crying and dancing, as we watched our beloved leader walk out of political imprisonment after 27 years, holding the hand of his wife, Winnie Mandela.

A few months later, we were invited to welcome the Mandelas at the Oakland International Airport, during their worldwide tour. As he walked down the steps of the plane, my little sister Noelene greeted Mr Mandela on the tarmac with flowers. Mr Mandela received the bouquet with a gracious kiss on each of Noelene's cheeks. Beaming with pride and uncontained joy, my mom exclaimed, "Noelene, it is okay if you never wash your face again!" Later that day, surrounded by dignitaries, we joined the mass choir, coordinated by the beautiful voices of freedom, the Vukani Mawethu choir, at the Oakland Coliseum. Dad fondly recalls:

"When Mr. Mandela visited the Bay area, I was standing and talking to a reporter, Dennis Richmond, not far from the podium at the Oakland Coliseum, when suddenly a large group of people surrounding Mr. and Mrs Mandela made their appearance on the way to the platform. For some reason unbeknown to me, Mr Mandela's eyes fell on me. Being a tall man he stretched himself over the security, offering to me his hand which I eagerly grabbed in warm greeting.

His wife, Mrs Winnie Mandela, did the same. I wondered, was I just fortunate that day, or was this providential?"

Some of us were college students at UC Berkeley and I had started writing a few articles for "The Daily Cal," the campus newspaper. As my dad recalls that momentous day, I too recall feeling so blessed to be in a small room of reporters that afternoon, with the Mandelas.

As if it were a dream, the torturous system of Apartheid was unraveling before our eyes ushering in the birth of a new democracy! South Africa announced its first democratic elections in 1994.

While I had the luxury of voting at the Courthouse in Oakland, California, one of many polling stations set up for South Africans in many cities around the world, lines of my fellow countrymen wrapped around polling stations in the cities and townships of South Africa. Voters waited for hours and hours to participate in this historic event. My husband, then fiancé, worked at the polls in Johannesburg. He fondly recalls watching an older woman vote for the first time. After a long time in line, she spent a long time in the voting booth and finally emerged with a little piece of paper, the size of a postage stamp, in her hand. She had torn Nelson Mandela's picture off the ballot and wanted to know where to paste the little picture, to cast her vote. Poll workers assisted her with a new ballot. In the months and years before, we had been denied access to the best beaches that were "reserved for whites" … and hotels, and restaurants and supervisory job positions. We had to get government consent to attend white universities. It was illegal for us to live in well cared for white neighborhoods, or to attend the beautiful white schools with updated facilities, or even marry outside of our race classification. Those who dared to protest were beaten and tortured and killed. On April 27th 1994 we went to the polls to vote Nelson Mandela, our childhood hero, into power and reclaim a piece of our humanity.

On November 4, 2008, the United States of America elected its first African American president! With a tear in my eye and a tremble in my soul, I watched the election results on TV that night. We kept our 5 and 7 year old children up later that night, to watch history in the making. Alec, our then 7 year old, had inquired months before, "Mom, is the brown man running for president?" When I said yes, in a firm, decisive voice he responded, "Then I hope he wins!"

"Why, Alec?"

"...because there are no brown presidents on the poster in my school library."

Regardless of race, millions have been inspired and re-energized by these elections, defining moments in world history!

16

NOORDGESIG (THE NORTHERN FACE OF SOWETO) MLAMLAMKUNZI

by Samuel Moonsamy

THE year was 1956, when as a young pastor, having completed my second year at Bible College, I was asked to become the Pastor of the Noordgesig "Coloured" church. At the end of the same year I also started a pastorate at the Lenasia Military Camp where 50 Indian families had been forcefully moved from Johannesburg, under the Group Areas Act. The Apartheid regime passed this Act for what they described as the "removal of the black spots" from the city. By doing this, the government was promoting the grand scheme of Apartheid, making way for white occupation of the best areas in and around the big cities. "Coloured" people were also considered non-entities like all the people of color in South Africa, and were placed in "Coloured" areas, under the Group Areas Act of 1950. Prior to that, they ("Coloureds," Indians and Blacks) had formed enclaves in Vrededorp, Fordsburg, Fereirastown, Doornfontein and a little further out in Albertville, Newclare and Noordgesig.

Noordgesig to the North of Soweto

Noordgesig, literally translated as "Northern Face," a town for "Coloured" people, is situated to the North of Soweto, the South Western Township. Further north, the yellow mountainous residue of soil from the gold mines, framed an area called Crown Mines near New Canada and Langlaagte. The golden leftovers of the gold mines evidenced the wealth of South Africa. The biggest slice of this wealth had always gone to privileged white South Africans, with barely any leftovers for those who labored to mine the precious metal.

During my tenure, the main road running from Soweto past Noordgesig was the main artery to the city of Gold, IGoli, lately named Gauteng Province. The main means of transportation were the SAR South African Railways and PUTCO (Public Utility Transport Corporation) with buses commonly known as Green Mamba. The concept of taxis known today was yet unknown then.

Young Africans who had no amusement and nothing to live for, in the depressing climate of Apartheid, rode the trains by "staff" meaning that they waited for the train to gain maximum speed, then they pounced on to the door handles hanging precariously before climbing in. These were the daredevil riders we saw daily who risked their lives for fun, and sometimes did not live to see the next day or moment, falling under the cruel rails. Young people from Noordgesig traveled mainly by bus which also had its risks and dangers.

The houses were small red brick buildings in uniform style with no bathrooms except for a toilet/outhouse in the backyard and also a tap (faucet) in the yard. Inside were the kitchen, dining room and two or three bedrooms with cement floors and the ever-present coal stoves that spewed up a plume of smoke in the mornings and the evenings when it was cooking time. The smoke created a dark, misty, fog-like substance over the entire township evoking a feeling of hopelessness and despair while in reality there was a suffocating smokescreen of which the general population was totally unaware.

I lived here on weekends with the Tracey family and slept on a mattress in the dining-room. They were a large family and had eight children at the time, later ten children, Louisa, Colin, Norman (late), Yvonne, Rhoda, Dennis, Martin, Linda, Sidney and Mark. When I was living with them, Linda was the baby. The other two were born after my time in the area. The very thought that this was such a large family, yet they had time and place for me, is difficult for me to comprehend. They were kind enough to take me in as a part of the family, and share with me their accommodation and food for a whole year. My earnings of R15 was paid out to Bible College fees and the balance of R5 was used for monthly expenses.

After the meetings on Sundays, we had dinner together with the Traceys. Some of the other church members also invited me home for dinner, which customarily was the main meal of the week. Families gathered around the table to share the roast beef, chicken and vegetables over rice and delicious gravy. Dessert was normally custard and jelly (jello) or delicious homemade "melk-tert" (milk-tart, similar to custard pie). In the mornings, before going to church on Sunday, we drank steaming cups of hot white tea (black tea with milk) with delicious "ḳoeksisters" (a tasty twisted doughnut-like treat, seasoned with warm spices such as cinnamon and nutmeg, quickly dipped in light syrup and covered in coconut) hot out of the oven, a delicacy introduced by the Cape Malays.

After dinner, I stayed over with the Traceys, who lived on Meyers Straat (Street). On Monday mornings, together with long lines of people, we took the bus to the city, to get to our Bible College van, a military truck which we had named, "Sally Sue."

Standing: Susan Ehrenreich, Mannie Tillicks, George Taylor, Sidney Holmes, Gwayne Challen, Sidney Fortoen, Jackie Cousins, Louis Jantjes Sitting: Billy Douman, George Meyers, Samuel Moonsamy

In the Steps of a Stalwart Preacher and Politician

Prior to my appointment as the new pastor, my predecessor was also my close friend and fellow student at Rehoboth Bible College, Pastor Godfrey Beck. He was a tall, handsome, extremely intelligent man. He was also an ex-serviceman who served in the last world war. Both he and George Taylor, my mentor and pastor, told of their experiences in the military and how they were accepted on a false declaration of their age which they made much older though they were younger. Godfrey told me that he was assigned with the military to take a consignment of horses to Egypt by ship. Academically he was ill equipped, with little or no formal education, and often told of his limited standard four education. Godfrey surmounted this shortcoming by self-education. When I asked him how he gained his education, he told me that it was largely through reading the newspapers, since libraries for non-whites, were few and far between. In most cities there were no libraries at all, for people of color.

Spiritual and Political Acumen

Under the leadership of Pastor Godfrey Beck, the church made great strides and was well on its way to becoming a self-sufficient, self-supporting organization. Unfortunately for the church, he left and instead became an astute political stalwart in the "Coloured" community, a voice that spoke for the "Coloured" people who were in deep political and spiritual distress and despair.

I knew that Godfrey Beck, pastor of the Noordgesig church, could be that spokesperson for "Coloured" people, a population with limited representation by a "Coloured People's Representative," ostensibly a white man, in a white parliament at Cape Town. By then, "Coloureds" in the Transvaal had absolutely no self-representation. Godfrey Beck, because of his political activism, was considered "persona non grata" in the "sacred" realm of the church, because his views ran counter to the government, whom the church did not want to offend. He also became a target in the eyes of the government, who had no respect for dissidents. At that time, the authorities were in a frantic mood to wipe out and extinguish any and all black activism.

Despite all of this, he was known to be a man of immeasurable courage, fortitude, and calm. He never minced words. This in itself brought a feeling of insecurity to the church that he may be considered a political "predikant" (preacher). His actions and aspirations were not acceptable to an American based church, ill prepared to take necessary risks, and interfere in the domestic affairs of a country set in its way, refusing to change.

The two of us held a similar view of the oppressive system in a church that was "apolitical" and totally unprepared to challenge the government on the painful issues facing its people of color. Godfrey was known to speak out against the system, much to the disdain of church authorities who wanted to steer clear of political engagement.

Mission to Kimberley Executed by his Leadership

As a student he applied himself with diligence, working hard to excel as the top student in the two years that I spent with him. He possessed a prodigious memory and unequaled presentation and persuasiveness within and among his counterparts, including college educated people. He spearheaded and organized a mission to Kimberley, together with the student body. We traveled at the back of the mid-sized military truck, "Sally Sue." We started the Diamond Fields Mission having open air and tent meetings at Barkley West, the two clothing manufacturing factories in the Floors Township. People in these areas were responding favorably to the 13 young men from Johannesburg. They also entertained us lavishly with local hospitality including Sullivan's Herb Beer, a non-alcoholic soda.

He presented his sermons well and articulated the Word of God with enthusiasm, candor, and deep inspiration. People looked up to him as a natural-born-leader and it was not unusual to see a full page article about him on the front pages of the more liberal newspaper, the Daily Mail. However, because of his strong stance against the government he was targeted by the Special Branch of the police and had to flee overnight to Botswana to ask for political asylum. After a few years in Botswana because of his criticism of the system, he was asked to leave and was delivered into the hands of the South African police at the border. I learned then from George Taylor that while in prison at the John Vorster Square he negotiated a deal to leave the country with the support of the United Nations and was exiled to Norway where his family joined him. It is believed that later he died in Norway. Though seriously handicapped by a hearing deficiency, he conducted his work meticulously, without complaint.

A New Pastor

In the shadow and footsteps of this man, I was called upon to fill the pastorate for which I felt infinitely ill prepared. Nevertheless, I accepted the challenge as Godfrey Beck was a personal friend and I hated to see his work not furthered.

I remember well on that first Sunday of January 1956, I was unceremoniously but warmly introduced to the people. They had gathered at the little chapel that seated roughly about 150 people, on the extreme southern end of the corner of the school yard. Those who were present were friendly and accommodating. That morning I had traveled by bus from Paardevlei to the train station at Kliptown. I then boarded a train headed for the city, via Nancefield, with Pimville in the West. I then went on to Orlando with Mlamlamkunzi as my final destination. I got off at the station and remember well a crudely written, insulting note at the little window where the tickets were to be purchased. I walked quickly along the pathway in the grass that led to the main road from the adjacent Orlando, crossing over into Noordgesig an area exclusively for "Coloureds." Rev. J.F. Penn the principal of the Bible College introduced me and then preached the sermon about the call of God.

Sometimes, I still picture the crudely written sign on cardboard stuck above the window where blacks stood, sometimes in long lines to purchase their tickets to the city and suburbs:

"IF YOU DO NOT KNOW HOW TO STAND
IN A STRAIGHT LINE WHEN BUYING
YOUR TICKETS, HOW WILL YOU RULE
YOURSELF IF YOU GET YOUR FREEDOM."

Small wonder one day when the weight of the people came crashing down, that the people, so angry, looted the ticket offices that lie crumbled to the ground and grabbed all the money and tickets. Little wonder that often the trains became the target of any uprising in the townships.

Overcrowded trains, plagued by crime, arrived at their own convenience, more often late. Serious accidents occurred because of train conductors lacking the patience to wait for everyone to board. Trains many times pulled away with people clambering on and struggling to board. Nobody, including the train officials, cared for the lives of old and young who tried to get on. Many died because of this gross and heartless negligence.

I am truly grateful to the people of Noordgesig who welcomed me with open arms. This is where I received an education about life, much more than any formal schooling could afford me.

17

SCHOOL DAYS IN SOUTH AFRICA

by Priscilla Moonsamy
daughter of Samuel and Sue Moonsamy

I LOOKED out of my classroom window, and was shocked to see a steady stream of uniformed policemen marching into our school with huge machine guns. I ran to tell the teacher and he rushed to lock our classroom door. Though panicked, we tried to remain calm but could hear the commotion outside. Students had been protesting the Apartheid system for several weeks and were now heading back to their classrooms. A few students still remained outside on the playground at our school and I was worried that my two younger sisters were still out there. As soon as things quieted a bit, we were allowed to leave the classroom, as it was the end of the school day. I ran to find Susheela and Ursula. With a flood of relief, I spotted them through a crowd of students and ran to them. Though I feared school from a very young age, this day was different.

When I started school in the first grade, mom would lay out my royal blue uniform at night. It had a deep red collar with a belt around the waist and multiple pleats on the skirt portion. I remember her folding the pleats so they would fit into each other before ironing it which took forever. I placed my pure white knee high socks and my clean underwear next to the ironed uniform, with my black freshly polished and shined shoes on the floor below. In the morning I would climb out of bed and start to get ready for school. Mom would braid my hair with two braids using a small rubber band to tie the ends. She had to cover the rubber bands with red ribbon because if they showed we would be in trouble at school.

Dad would insist that we eat breakfast before we left for school each morning. He'd cook the jungle oats (oatmeal) early in the morning on our coal stove, and serve it warm in a bowl with some milk and sugar. He would often relate funny stories to us around the table. He said that as a toddler I would wake up and find him on his knees praying by his bed early in the morning. I would climb up over his shoes on to his calves, pull his head backwards by his hair, and pry open his eyes, to see what in the world he was doing. He also told how on one occasion he was about to deliver his sermon at church, when he started flipping through the pages frantically looking for the scripture he was about to read. He had to borrow someone's bible to find and read the passage. Later at home, they found the remains of a chewed-up page scattered all over the living room. He laughed and told mom, "we need to follow the example of our 2 yr old, she takes the words of Jeremiah 15:16

very literally: *"Thy words were found and I did eat them; and thy word was unto me the joy and rejoicing of mine heart."*

Probably because of their abject poverty growing up, mom and dad also made certain that we had lunch every day, which usually was a sandwich made with two slices of bread spread with butter and topped with cheese and sliced tomato. Some days we would buy potato crisps (a bag of chips) at school, and layer it on our sandwich to add some crunchy flavor. Yum!

On a cold morning in the first grade, I watched as dad turned the key in the ignition, but our car would not start. My heart sank. There was not sufficient time to walk to school. He tried and tried and to my relief, it finally started. "I think I could still make it dad, let's go quickly!" I heard the bell ring as the car pulled up to the gate. Dad said "run, you will make it," and slowly pulled away, thinking that I had just made it in time. I ran panting, as fast as my 6 year old legs could carry me, with the cold air rushing through my lungs. The prefect (student hall monitor) standing at the gate, motioned me with his hand to stop and then said, "You are late." With other latecomers the prefect marched us to the office. We each got 6 painful lashes on our hands with a bamboo cane. I walked to my class in tears. My teacher was a very kind lady and she comforted me and gave me some water to drink.

When my sister Susheela was beaten by a teacher and had a blood clot under her finger nail, mom was livid. She went to the principal and told him firmly "your teacher assaulted my child!" The teacher later told Susheela that she should not have "carried tales," which meant that "what happened in class stayed in class." Young Susheela, only 7 at the time, confidently responded, "my mom and dad always tell me that I should share everything with them, so I will continue to tell them everything that happens in school."

On another occasion, Susheela was ill and was not able to turn in her essay assignment on time. I remember her staying up all night to complete her handwritten assignment. The following day, because her essay was late, the teacher crumpled up the essay without looking at it, and threw it into the fire in the little coal stove in the classroom.

Today Susheela works as a high school counselor in Oakland and helps many students.

Despite the negative experiences, we also had wonderful teachers in South Africa, who were very committed to their calling. They inspired us to overcome obstacles and reach goals that we did not think were reachable.

Apparently it was much worse during my parents schooling. Here is an excerpt my dad posted recently on social media as a response to a post about school beatings:

"SCHOOL BEATINGS BRING BACK HORRIFIC AND SAD, SAD, SAD, MEMORIES TO ME PERSONALLY. EDUCATION RUINED BY BRUTALITY.

Cruel, humiliating, wicked. Reminds me of what we had to endure as kids. The most fearful and hated thing in my life was school. I hated every day of school life. The crimes we committed were: being absent without a doctor's letter; uncut nails; being late; not handing in homework; clothes not clean; making a noise in class; being inattentive; writing poorly; not knowing the multiplication tables. On one occasion a teacher became angry because I accidentally wiped off the black board, he beat me until blood came oozing down my

*one leg. On another occasion I passed out
because while being beaten, I hit my head
against the wall and fainted. Absolutely no
known law to protect me as a kid. Sadly, we
were part and parcel of a skewed system."*

My second grade teacher was excellent at keeping a class
of 7 year olds silent. She did not tolerate any talking in class
and if she heard any slight chattering even by one or two kids,
she would make the entire class stand and give each child a
lashing on our hands with a bamboo cane, which she carried
around often. Though I was a good student, I was extremely
shy. She found great pleasure in having the shiest boy in class
sit next to me and hold my hand or kiss me on my cheek. She
thought this was hilarious and laughed hysterically, while I
wished I could disappear through the floor.

A couple of times a year, nurses would visit our school to
administer vaccinations (shots). This same teacher would tell
the kids they needed to queue up for candy or ice-cream and,
lo and behold, it was really for vaccinations! I hated needles
and I would sometimes faint when I needed to get shots. It
was so scary as a kid to line up at school with queues of nervous
kids all around. On one occasion, we were all almost in tears
as we lined up, but were pleasantly surprised to find that there
was actually an ice-cream combi (van) outside. It was in fact
the same one that had come to my dad's vacation bible school
(VBS) a few weeks prior at our church, which was located right
next to my school. We learned that the owner of the ice-cream
truck had collapsed while selling ice-cream one day and a kid
had run to get him help. He believed that his life was saved
that day and wanted to thank the kid that saved him. He never
learned which child had helped him that day, so he went to

every school in our neighborhood and even to our church, to hand out free ice-cream. I lucked out, I got ice-cream twice!

Ice-cream combi (van) at Vacation Bible School at church, with Alpha Primary School in the background: July, 1973

Now in standard 10 (12th grade) in high school, on this day of protest, the only vans we could see were cop vans. The police tried to surround the kids remaining from the student protest but the kids quickly ran into the last wing of the school. The cops then surrounded that entire wing and marched all of the students and teachers out into police vans, including the ones that just happened to be in those classrooms at the time; some had no involvement in the boycotts that day. Parents came rushing to the school, some in desperation when they could not find their kids.

We stood trembling as we watched. We could hear the

students locked in the back of the vans singing, to the tune of the anthem at the time:

"From the hearts of starving children
to the malnutrition bound
From the banned on Robben Island
to the chained in Africa
We will never be subservient
to the things that hold us down
We will fight for all Black people,
Africa our own dear land."

In between the singing, we could hear the loud intermittent sounds of gun barrels pointed at the kids, scraping across the sides of the grating on the enclosed trucks to intimidate and silence the kids inside. Some kids were crying, but despite their grave situation, their spirits were not crushed. In a couple of days some of the kids that had been driven away in those army trucks returned to school. Some had bandages on their legs or arms. No one said much. I heard from my friends that those taken were interrogated at the prison. The leaders when found were held for a longer time, but everyone was mostly silent about the details. Some of the parents who were lawyers helped get the students back home.

I was fortunate to end 12th grade with a matriculation exemption (university entrance pass) with several others in my class. I entered an Indian University in Durban while I waited to hear whether I would get permission from the government to attend the white University of the Witwatersrand. This university was much closer to home, internationally accepted, and also offered the pre-medical degree that I was interested in pursuing.

I became interested in the health field as a young child

Miss P. Moonsamy
P.O. Box 454
LENASIA
1820

1980 -09- 1 7

Madam

CONSENT TO ATTEND A UNIVERSITY IN TERMS OF SECTION 31
OF ACT 45 OF 1959

1.   The Minister of Indian Affairs has approved your appli-
      cation to attend the University of the Witwatersrand
      to follow the course B.Sc Med.

2.   The certificate of consent is attached and should be
      handed to the University authorities when you apply
      for admission.

Yours faithfully

SECRETARY FOR INDIAN AFFAIRS

Consent received by me to attend a white University. All students of
color had to apply and provide strong justification. A small
percentage of students were granted permission.

when I was treated at a local clinic by a kind lady. As I walked
home holding my mom's hand that day, I asked her "Mom,
who was that lady? Was she a nurse?" Mom replied "She was
the doctor, darling." "Really mom, can women also become

doctors?" I asked. I had never seen a female doctor before. My mom smiled and said "Yes my dear child, women can become doctors or anything that they put their minds to." I replied, "Mom, one day I really want to be a doctor like that kind lady." I did not become a doctor, but I did end up becoming a scientist, working in healthcare developing patient-related genetic and oncology diagnostic assays, at least a field where I felt I was still helping patients.

When I eventually received permission to attend the University of the Witwatersrand, I was happy to transfer back closer to home. My sister Susheela received permission to the same university a year later but with many conditions, including no guarantee of bursaries (scholarships) or a teaching job in a public school after graduation. These conditions clearly were meant to dissuade her from attending a white university. She decided to attend despite the conditions.

I traveled by bus from Lenasia, which took about an hour or more to the campus daily. My parents and I decided to ask for permission for me to reside in the dormitory even though it was for whites only. To my surprise I was given consent to live in the dormitory with a few other students of color. After only one semester, all students of color were asked to leave the dorm, without explanation. Not wanting to give up, my parents and I went to another dorm. A very kind lady in dorm admissions decided to go against the policy of the State and allow me and a few other students of color residence there. I lived there for a few months and then the same lady, with tears in her eyes, told us that though we had done nothing wrong, some of the white students had complained because they did not want to live in the same dorm with students of color. Once again, I was back on my long commute from home. Despite these conditions, many of the students I travelled with, have become leaders in the community and around the world.

When we moved to the USA, I was very excited to gain acceptance to the University of California at Berkeley. In awe, I found that some of my professors had authored the heavy books that I had carried over all of those miles, afraid that I would not find these in the vast USA. I was grateful to graduate from UC Berkeley with a Genetics degree, the same field of study I had started in South Africa. I am truly grateful for my parents' sacrificial love. They fought so hard to give us more opportunities and a better life.

The first 5 siblings, with the 3 oldest in our school uniforms.

18

Diamonds in Our Rich Red African Soil

by Noelene and Neil Moonsamy
children of Samuel and Sue Moonsamy

M Y sister Susheela, who was 10 years older than me, had just graduated from high school and was in a teacher's training college, when I was in the 2nd grade. At the time, there was a shortage of teachers in the school system, and since Susheela was in training, she was recruited to teach at our school while studying. She became my 2nd grade teacher, and I had to call her Madam. We had to address female teachers as "Madam" and male teachers as "Sir." When she entered the class, we would all stand and sing in unison, as we did with all our teachers "Good Morning Madam Moonsamy." Having my older sister as my teacher came with some privileges. It meant that I could write on the board after school while I waited for her to finish her work so we could walk home together. During class, I would try to get away with some extra privileges as well, "Madam, can I write on the board?" "No Noelene, not now." "Madam, can I pleeeease write on the board?" "Noelene NO!" "Susheela, if you don't let me write on the board, I will tell mommy!"

Our brother Neil attended the same school. He was two years older than me, and in the fourth grade. That year was Neil's 10th birthday. On August 8th, 1982 we had the biggest party we had ever had at our home. I was 7, almost 8 years old. A few days prior, we both walked to our school together in the morning. As usual, we ran off to our separate classrooms. After school I played with my friends, then walked home. When I got home, Susheela asked if I had seen Neil, because he was not home yet. I responded that the last time I had seen him was when we parted ways in the morning. It was still early in the day, and we knew that he would be home soon. Perhaps he was around the corner with our cousin Thyran, or with his neighborhood friends. When Melanie and Ursula got home from school, we ran together to all of his friends homes in the neighborhood, to see if we could find him. His classmate Rodney, who was nearby, said that he went to the bathroom in second period and never returned. The teacher threatened to give him "six of the best," which meant six whips with a cane.

This was nothing unusual for us. Even the most well be-haved kids got whipped in school. We were often told by our teachers not to tell our parents. We did, at times, when we came home crying, with red marks on our hands, and mom would complain to the school. However, we had to be back in the classroom, with the same teacher that would be upset that we had complained. It was a no-win situation. For our punishment, the boys would have to bend over, to be whipped on their behinds. The girls would receive lashes on the palms of their hands. I remember the boys trying to wear extra shorts underneath their grey school pants to avoid the sting of the cane, while us girls had nothing to shield our bare hands. In the first grade, I remember seeing a teacher break a pen on a child's head by hitting the child over and over on her head.

We later learned that Neil had forgotten to do his homework. Afraid of the punishment, he had asked to be excused to go to the restroom, but never returned. The teacher assumed Neil had run home and did not think it was necessary to inform anyone. When we could not find Neil, we called our parents, who were away for a few days at a church conference. They immediately started heading back home, but were over an hour's drive away in heavy traffic. Together with some of Neil's classmates, we kept searching at nearby house shops and fields, to no avail.

As the news spread of Neil's disappearance, our extended family, neighbors and friends all started coming over to our place, to see how they could help. When mom and dad arrived home, there was still no trace of Neil. Mom was crying hysterically. Her hysteria resurfaced with each face that came through the door that night. Our doors were open all night, and search parties were in and out of our home as friends and family stayed to help. Someone said they saw two boys walking toward the hills. Another person said that he had seen a child with the description of my brother in a store in the opposite direction. Dr. Budhia, our local physician, came over to give my mom something to calm her down. The school principal and teacher that had threatened to beat my brother, nervously walked into our house.

My mother looked at them in pain and yelled, "If anything

were to happen to my child, I will personally hold you and your school responsible!" We all became increasingly concerned as it got darker and colder outside. Nobody slept that night, the lights stayed on all night. The entire neighborhood was awake as people formed human chains to walk through the hills searching for Neil.

Neil and I were inseparable as kids. We argued, we fought, and oftentimes our parents had to discipline us. When my mom would hear us argue, she would say "there goes Britain and Argentina again," since the two countries were at war over the Falkland Islands at the time. Mom had a calendar on the kitchen wall with a picture of Jesus on it. While arguing one morning, mom came into the kitchen, and asked what the matter was now. I said "Mommy, I am mad at Neil because he dropped my spoon on the floor!" to which he responded that he did not, and I said "Yes you did!" As we bickered back and forth, in frustration I pointed to the calendar and said "Mom ask Jesus what happened, He saw the whole thing."

Neil was very active and would play outside all day with his friends. They would climb trees, and run around the neighborhood playing cops and robbers. He had longer eyelashes than all 5 of his sisters. People would often comment that he had beautiful eyelashes. He hated that, as he did not want anything on him to be considered beautiful. After all, girls were beautiful, but boys were tough. One day, he got a pair of scissors and cut off his eyelashes. Thankfully, he did not injure his eyelid, but you can imagine how furious mom was, when she found out.

When I was born, Neil was unhappy to have yet another sister. But soon he realized that I could keep up with everything he did, as I tried to follow in the footsteps of my big brother. I looked up to him so much, as I still do today, even though

I will never admit it. I became Neil's little sidekick. Though we fought a lot, he always stood up for me and protected me. When his friends did not want to play with girls, Neil said very firmly to them: "If she doesn't play, I don't play." They would reluctantly let me join in, and pretty soon, I was accepted as one of them.

Sometimes we would eavesdrop on our older sisters' phone conversations. Neil would sneak a hose pipe under their bedroom doors with a funnel on the end that we held over our ears, while listening and quietly giggling, hiding in the adjacent room. They wondered how we knew what they had talked about when we sometimes accidentally repeated incidents from their phone conversations. One time, we pretended that we were fighting, and I said "Mom, Neil pinched me!" instead of the usual "I didn't do it" response, Neil echoed "Mom, I pinched Noelene." My parents both yelled down the hallway, "You two stop fighting!"...as we giggled in the room, knowing that they did not realize that we were actually in agreement, just teasing them.

So where was my brother now?!

The next morning, my dad was exhausted and at the end of his rope, after driving through surrounding cities and towns all night, only stopping at pay phones to call home, to check if anyone had found Neil, and to ask for leads. My older sisters answered the phone and spoke to dad, and the myriad of other callers. Mom was unable to answer the phone; she was inconsolable. With every call, she would look up with a glimmer of hope in her eyes, praying for good news. The next morning, it was crisp and sunny, yet it felt very gloomy to us, we all went around searching again. My dad and his friend's son, were slowly driving through our neighborhood when they spotted a little boy. It was Neil! He was playing in the red dust of a sand hill, with two other little boys, less than two miles from our home near an abandoned car. My dad thought he was dreaming, or that his eyes were playing tricks on him, because of the lack of sleep, and the scary thoughts going through his mind. He jumped out of the car and quickly collected the three boys and drove them home. When mom heard the news, she immediately ran out, crying with relief. In thankfulness to God, she embraced her son.

Neil's rendition of the events

"It must have been really hot in Africa" was something I would hear over and over when our family arrived in the USA. The typical images of Africans toiling away in the hot deserts of North Africa or in the sweltering heat of the equator was something we never experienced in the relatively temperate climate in Johannesburg, South Africa. Oh but our frigid, cold winters was something I had never seen portrayed in any western media. Children bundled in hats and gloves walking across the frost covered grass is not the first image that comes to mind when westerners think of Africa.

When I jumped out of the warm bed in the morning, as my feet touched the icy cold tiled concrete floors it was jarring, to say the least, and felt as if it was sending shock waves of cold throughout my entire body. I would run to the bathroom to fight with my sisters for space at our one bathroom sink. Being the only boy with 5 sisters and one bathroom to share was the never ending agony of my childhood. I remember crying outside the bathroom as my older sisters, then teenagers, would get ready. I sometimes even had to resort to peeing in the backyard. Other little boys wanted toys like bikes or cars, but when I was young, all I wanted was my own bathroom.

When I eventually accessed the bathroom, I would wash so quickly with the water barely touching my body, brush my teeth and rush back into the room where our upright asbestos heater would radiate some warmth. We would hang our clothes over the heater to warm it up a bit and it felt amazing to pull the warm socks over my icy feet. We quickly gulped down some hot tea with milk and sugar along with some toast or cereal with hot milk, which we called porridge. I still remember our favorite brand of oatmeal was called "jungle oats," fitting for the concrete jungle of Johannesburg. We were always rushing off to school in the morning. You did not want to be late for school.

I hated school. If you were a minute late, you would get whipped with a cane. There were a myriad of reasons to get whipped in our schools: forgot your pen, pencil or ruler? You would get whipped. Forgot your white gym shorts? You would get whipped. Talked out of turn in class? You would get whipped. Untidy handwriting, "dog ears" on your textbook, or workbook, forgot your handkerchief, having unclipped fingernails, girls could not even wear the wrong colored ribbon in their hair! Then, of course, there were "legitimate" reasons we got whipped, like performing poorly on a test, or not doing our homework. And...that's where my school experience could have been a bit easier, but you see, I was and still am a terminal procrastinator. At age 9 I was a playful absent minded child. When I was playing outside, my mind would drift to distant places from any or all of my responsibilities. I didn't even want to come in to eat. My family would tease and say that some parents punished their children by letting them go to bed without dinner. For me, being dragged away from my ever important playing to have to do a mundane activity like eat, was a punishment. They would jokingly call outside when dinner was ready for me to come in and get my punishment. After a long day of playing and then dinner and a bath, I would doze off to sleep with homework being the furthest thing from my mind. It was only in the morning when I woke up that I had this sinking feeling in my stomach. "I'm really sick today," I would plead with my parents to let me stay home, but my dad could see right through my lies and would insist I get up and go to school. My mum, who would also see through my obviously fake stomach pain or headache, would sometimes have pity on me and allow me to stay home some days. I would be so happy and play all day not doing my homework again, just putting off my whipping for another day.

It was a typical winter morning when my particularly agitated second period Afrikaans teacher walked into class. The entire class stood up as we were required to do, as each teacher walked in and we said "Goeie more meneer" (Good morning sir). English and Afrikaans were two languages required by the South African government at the time. If you failed one of your languages you would be held back a year even if you were a genius in other subjects. "If any of you didn't do your homework today, you are in big trouble," my teacher yelled holding his long bamboo cane in his hand. I looked down at my obviously empty notebook and froze with fear. This was not a good day to have forgotten to do my homework.

I nervously raised my hand, "Yes Neil, what do you want?" my teacher asked. "Can I please go to the bathroom, Sir?" I replied. He nodded his head in affirmation and I quickly headed outside toward the bathroom. I saw the school principal rounding the corner towards his office; without much thought I headed in the opposite direction of the bathrooms toward the playground and made a frantic dash, hoping nobody would see me. Without looking back, I ran as fast as I could towards the 6 foot high metal fence. I jumped, grabbing the top of the fence, and in one motion catapulted my skinny body over the metal fence. My grey school uniform pants got snagged on the hooks and ripped as I landed feet first outside the school yard. I ran like I never ran before, expecting the principal and teachers clambering over the fence, racing towards me with canes in hand, closing in on me. I looked back and nobody was there. I had escaped unseen. So I turned and continued to run and run and run across the open veld (field).

In the distance I saw a grove of eucalyptus trees. I headed for the cover of the trees to have a place to hide in case the teachers came out looking for me. I heard a rustling in the bushes as I slowly approached and thought it might be some animals, but to my surprise, two boys emerged. One seemed a few years older than me and the younger one seemed closer to my age. "What are you running from?" the older boy asked me. I told them the story and they immediately said not to worry, and that they would protect me. The older boy had a few shaving blades in his pocket, and they put them on the sticks from the veld making makeshift weapons. Swinging them back and forth, they were able to slice some of the tall grass down. "If your teacher comes here, we will chop him with our weapons," they said, "don't worry we won't let him get you."

I didn't even ask where they were from or what they were doing out here in the veld, but I was glad to have found some company. I later found out they were brothers and they had an older married sister not far from there. They asked me if I had any money, and I had 50 cents in my pocket which I usually got from my parents to buy something at the school tuck shop (snack stand), usually a bag of chips and something to drink. We walked along to a local "house shop" where to my surprise, instead of buying candy which is what I would have done, they bought some bread and milk and we shared the bread and passed the small carton of milk around.

"So do you want to go home?" they asked. I did not want to go home, fearing the teachers would come looking for me. So I looked up over the horizon toward the hills away from the town we lived in. I suggested that we head up that way. The two brothers agreed, so we started heading toward the hills. After what seemed like hours of walking we arrived at the foot of the hills, dusty, with my school sweater covered in sticky prickly blackjacks, the seeds from the hardy weed that covered the veld. When we started to hike up towards the hills we were surprised to see a few mud huts with some black African people living up there. They curiously looked at the unfamiliar sight of these three school boys hiking by – they greeted and did not seem bothered by us as we walked by.

As the sun began to drop behind the horizon, it got darker and colder. All of a sudden reality hit and I became afraid and was ready to go home, but it was getting too dark and dangerous to make it back to my house, so we headed back towards the flats (apartment building), where the boys had known of an abandoned car nearby. We set up camp near the car and huddled together as the older boy made a fire in a little drum next to the car. To my 9 year old mind, my parents were away at a church conference for a few days so I did not think they would be worried about me. I was cold, and I was now hungry and longed for the "punishment" of the warm meal at home. We climbed into the abandoned car and eventually I fell asleep.

I woke up in the morning and we began to play on the mound of construction gravel nearby, and to my surprise I saw my dad's car drive up. When he took me to the house along with my two new friends, I was surprised to see the commotion. All my sisters were home, together with my aunts, uncles, and church people. I didn't even realize they would all be so worried about me. I mean, I was 9 years old already, practically a grown man.

The Brother Returned (by Noelene Moonsamy)

Everyone was silent, with their eyes fixed on the three boys as they walked into the house. My grandmother, Huma, who lived with us and helped raise us, sprung into action. She never admitted it, but Neil was her favorite. We teased her about it, but she just laughed. She stepped between my dad, her son, and the boys before he could reprimand Neil, and quickly said, "Neil, bring your friends and follow me to the kitchen. You must be starved." They nodded obediently and quickly followed Huma. She poured three large bowls of cereal and milk and set them on the table. It was as if time was standing still, as we all watched the three boys sit and hastily eat. We felt amazing relief. The boys seemed oblivious to the grief and anguish that was caused. The realization that Neil really was home, after that traumatic night, began to settle over everyone. Family, friends, and neighbors smiled through their tears as they watched the three boys gulp down large spoonfuls of cereal. I, being so young, didn't quite grasp the seriousness of the situation, broke the silence when I looked at everyone and asked loudly, "Are we all supposed to cry now?" causing everyone through their tears to break into laughter.

Neil had spent the night outdoors with his two guardian angels. The older boy had made a fire in an old drum outside, near the old abandoned car. They took shelter there with Neil, staying true to their promise to protect him, as they each took turns keeping watch while the other two slept through the dangers lurking all around. Angels keeping watch. Diamonds in our rich red African soil.

Neil and Noelene

19

CHARIOTS OF FIRE

by Samuel Moonsamy

THE all encompassing tentacles of Apartheid had its grip over every aspect of our lives. To save face with the overseas media, and to give a false appearance of acceptance and accommodation, people of color from other countries, mainly Black Europeans and African Americans were allowed certain amenities such as public transportation or movie theatres.

South Africans of color were definitely not offered the same courtesy but sometime in the early eighties, we managed to circumvent the strict laws of Apartheid by attending a "white" movie theatre in Johannesburg, where no local blacks were allowed.

The movie "Chariots of Fire" was showing but not in any of the non-white theatres that we knew of in our area. Being in ministry, we were keen to watch this particular movie, because it also showed how a soon to be mission worker, born in China, of Scottish parents won the fastest mile and gained a gold medal in 1924.

I took the chance of calling the manager of a Johannesburg "whites only" movie theatre and remarkably he was sympathetic towards us and told us that he would allow us to attend. Elated and extremely excited I called our friends Pastor Gwayne and his wife Doreen Challen and asked them to attend this movie with us. With trepidation he agreed and all four of us were on our way to the "whites only" theatre worried that we still may not be accepted. We arrived early, so fortunately, no one else was in line at the box office, otherwise there may have been resistance against us as non-whites.

Ironically, the lady at the box office, whom I doubt was ever allowed in the theatre, asked for our passports which we did not have with us. Then, she called the manager who evidently told her that we should be allowed to attend as his guests. We tendered the amount she requested, and proceeded to take our seats, completely flabbergasted, shocked and fearful. As Doreen reminded us in Afrikaans, "Jong as die kerk mense uitvind, dan skop hulle ons uit." If the church hears about this, we will be kicked out of the church. We were in fear of both sides of the spectrum, the government and the church.

Had anybody complained or called the police then we stood the chance of being ousted or even imprisoned for sitting in a theatre other than one for our own race group. However, nothing of this sort happened and people around us seemed comfortable with us, apparently under the impression that we were foreigners visiting from London or America.

We watched the movie and were thrilled to see the person acting as Eric Liddell, run the fastest mile. His timing, I believe, was only a second behind that of Usain Bolt, and he captured a gold medal at the Paris Olympics in 1924. What a feat of endurance and what a great accomplishment of this young person.

I recalled the time when television was first broadcast in South Africa. We first bought a small black and white TV. I remember watching one day and there were absolutely no people of color on the television. I picked up the phone and called the South African Broadcasting Company and politely said, "I just bought a black and white TV but all I see is white," much to the fear and trepidation of my wife and kids. They were afraid that I would be traced and imprisoned for making such comments.

Shortly after, Cliff Richard, a famous British singer appeared on television on a kids program. Knowing the situation in South Africa, he specifically asked if he could have kids of color on his show. Because Cliff Richard was very popular in South Africa at the time, the producers obliged. As a pastor from an Indian Township, they called me and asked if I could arrange for a group of kids to appear on the show. I arranged for the children of local pastors to go to the television recording studio. It was such a privilege to meet Cliff Richard and for the children to be on a television program with him, most likely the first time a kids multiracial program was ever screened. Later I was asked to read the bible on television as the evening programming would open and close with a bible reading and prayer in a segment called "From the Book." Our kids were also asked to open with a song.

I also recalled how Billy Graham was invited to South Africa to speak at a huge stadium. He said he would only visit if the event was totally multiracial. It was one of the biggest events and one of the very first multiracial events of this size during the height of Apartheid. It was admirable that he was able to take this stand, not knowing that someday the walls of Apartheid would come crumbling down. I was invited to be on the panel of ministers who welcomed him at the event. He did not hold back in his talk regarding the issues of racism, small steps towards bigger changes that would occur later.

As we left the theater that day, we realized that for a moment in time we were oblivious of the church and the government. Our previous church, was strongly opposed to the movies as this was considered "worldly" and of a bad and immoral influence. We were told that even Christian movies made by Hollywood would finance other evil, immoral, and violent movies. We could be considered "backsliders" who would suffer disciplinary action or even ex-communication from the church. For years we had not gone to the movies believing our superiors that it was a sin, and we even taught this to our congregation. However, when we moved and started to work non-denominationally, we realized how important it was to have love in our hearts for God and others rather than enforce a bunch of petty rules that make people hypocritical and judgmental of others.

By segregating movie theaters and other public spaces, the government was making certain that the races in South Africa did not mix. Like someone has said, if you mix colors like blue and yellow, it will produce green, and of course mixing black and white would make grey, but in South Africa they say: "If you mix black and white, you'll get six months." This, according to the law, was the sentence to be applied for those who married across the color line.

That day we were exuberantly happy that we prevailed against both church and state, promising that we would keep our exploits a secret eternally. However, word did somehow get out and we heard that church leaders held meetings to discuss our attendance at the movie theatre. Though we were no longer associated with the group that enforced these laws, the long term effects still lingered.

Eventually, both church and state changed their policies regarding the laws we broke of "God and man." What was sin then is no more sin, and Apartheid, doomed to failure, is now a part of history, a bad dream, or worse, a nightmare, though still a reality that shaped and affected our lives today.

20

My Own Bathroom

told by Sue Moonsamy
written by her daughter Ursula Moonsamy

O NE evening in Yuba City, California, while we were all sitting around the dinner table, we asked our children what they would like for Christmas, since the season was fast approaching. Neil was first to respond: "My own bathroom..... so I would not have to spend most of my life waiting outside the bathroom for one of my sisters!" Everyone started laughing in response to our quick witted son.

Our youngest child, Noelene, chimed in, "I have a special bathroom for you, Neil. You can have any of the awful restrooms at the back of those gas stations that we used to see whenever we traveled to Durban." When our children were still little, for our vacations in South Africa, we would take our kids to the city of Durban by the warm Indian Ocean, a tropical paradise with white sandy beaches. We would drive to Durban, about 400 miles from Johannesburg, and spend a few days at Sam's uncle's home there. They were gracious enough to have us stay with them on our vacations, because hotels would have been expensive for a family of our size and we knew of no hotels, for people of color anyway.

For our road trips we always packed food to eat on the way. This not only helped with the expense of food on the trip, but we were also not allowed to eat inside the restaurants at the rest stops and I certainly did not want to buy from a window. On one particular occasion, when we stopped at a gas station, a couple of the kids got out of the car and ran into the restroom. They returned in tears saying that a lady in there had yelled at them harshly and told them to go to the restroom at the back. When they went to the back of the gas station, there was a filthy restroom that was not taken care of, with a "non-white" sign on it. On this occasion we decided to stop on the side of the road, and have them go behind some bushes instead. I remember listening to their conversations in the back of the car as we continued on our journey. Ursula had a clever idea to take revenge. She told her siblings with a smirk that when she grew up, she was going to build her own gas station and have a spotless restroom in the front for "non-whites" and a deliberately filthy, unserviced restroom for "whites only" in the back.

Sam explained to them that these laws were sinful, and that we were not to repay evil with evil, but rather that we would pray and work for change in our land. On ensuing trips our children now understood the system, and knew that I would defy it. They would wait for me and we would all go into the white restroom together. On one occasion there was a black lady hired to clean the white restrooms and to ask people of color to leave. I spoke to her kindly and told her that I understood that she needed the job. I asked her to call her manager so that he could come inside the ladies room and ask us to leave. By the time she came back we had already used the clean restroom and were on our way. I doubt that the manager ever showed. On busy long weekends, there would be lines at the rest stops to use the restroom. I would go and stand with my girls in line with all of the white ladies and though we would get hateful stares, I would encourage my children to use the restroom anyway in this hostile environment. Sam would wait with the "getaway" car ready to take off as soon as we were done, so that no one would have enough time to call the police. When the sign posted said "Europeans Only," a convenient term used in South Africa for whites, as a facade to deceive internationals, I would tell them I was from Europe. Fortunately there were no cell phones then, or I might have been imprisoned. Sam and I wanted our children to know what was happening in our country. We also wanted them to know that they were not inferior and that the experiences that we were facing in the country were no fault of theirs, or ours. Had we sheltered them and taken them into the non-white restrooms without a fight, they may have believed that they were inferior.

The dinner conversation took my mind even further back to my first office job in the city of Johannesburg in the early 1970's. I began to relate the story to my children.

I found myself in a job for which I was not qualified, but I knew that I had to learn quickly and perform well, so that we could provide for our four children at that time. The church expected my husband Sam to provide for our family on a salary of 35 rands a month, and forbade him to find other work, assuring him that his reward would be in heaven. Though they could not pay a living wage, church leaders made the ministers feel like they were out of the will of God if they did anything other than work full time for the church.

This particular job advertised in the newspaper, in the city of Johannesburg, was one of the few that did not specify that it was for 'Whites Only.' "Help Wanted" newspaper advertisements usually requested employees in black and white (no pun intended) with the required race specified, "Whites Only May Apply" or "Europeans Only." Sometimes it would state, "Regret, not for Non-Whites." The listing for this position did not specify a race. I called, not mentioning my last name so that my race would not be easily identified, and was told to come in to apply for the position.

The next day, I dressed in the best outfit I owned, and took the bus into the city of Johannesburg to apply for the position. I nervously walked down Loveday Street on a crisp but sunny morning, rehearsing what I needed to say to emphasize my abilities at the interview. I entered the tall building and took the elevator to the floor I needed, that opened up to a very elegant reception area. I smiled, and with confidence introduced myself, letting the receptionist know that I was there to apply for the position that was advertised in the newspaper. She looked at me confused and asked who told me to come in. I gave her the name of the person I had talked with on the phone and she went back to check. She returned and said that she was sorry to inform me that the position had been filled. Noticing my disappointment, the lady seemed to feel pity for me and asked how she could contact me if anything became available. I walked out with a heavy heart, because this was one of the few jobs in the newspaper that did not specify a required race, and for some reason I believed that I was the ideal candidate for the job.

To my surprise, a few days later, since we did not have a home phone, I received a telegram to come back into this office. I returned and learned that the person hired was overwhelmed by the demands of the job and had decided to walk out. At the interview I prayed that they would not ask about my education, since I did not have the opportunity to even attend high school. Instead, I had worked long hours from the age of thirteen in a clothing factory, snipping cottons off school uniforms. With enthusiasm and passion, I told the interviewer how I was willing and eager to learn and promised that if hired, I would do my very best. I did not know what to expect, but breathed a sigh of relief, when I was told immediately after the interview, that I was hired!

My desk was in a corner of the office in a little cubicle. On my first day at work, the manager came in and showed me the task he needed me to perform. There were little chips on copper wire that had to be soldered in a certain sequence onto a gold plaque. He slowly explained the process to me and then left me on my own to complete the first board. I was so nervous, and it all looked so confusing to me. I closed my eyes and said "Lord you know that I need this job, please help me." I opened my eyes and things started to make sense. After I was done, the manager came in to test the board. He found that I had made only two mistakes and was overjoyed. I learned that the previous hire had left in frustration after making up to 24 mistakes at her attempts on this task. The manager showed me how to remove and reapply the chips to fix my two errors, and once that was done, he tested the board on the mini computer and to my delight, it worked! Imagine my joy and relief as the board lit up before my eyes. The manager was so pleased. He congratulated me and told me that several employees had tried this task without success. I was so thankful to God that

He intervened that day. I felt so fortunate, to get a job usually unavailable to people of color.

When I look back, I cannot believe that I was learning to wire a program onto a computer. Prior to this, I had never even heard the word "computer." By no means did the large machine resemble any of our modern computers today. I was the only person of color in the office with well dressed white women and men working all around in different sections, with me far away, tucked in my little corner. Occasionally, one of them would look at me and smile, a bit intrigued by what I was doing. Most of them did not know how to perform my job, but did not want me to know this, for after all it was the general consensus that whites were more intelligent than people of color.

While working there, I fully complied with the rules, regulations and laws of Apartheid and at all times kept away from the locker room which I knew was for whites only. I also kept away from the dining area. Occasionally one of the fellow workers would talk to me. They would ask about my family and our lives in the Indian area of Lenasia. All of them told how they loved Indian curry and especially samoosas, a delicious paper-thin triangular pastry filled with ground meat or curried vegetables. Some of them were keen to learn about the non-white races and asked a lot about the way Indians lived. They were always shocked that Indians were people like them, with families, that had to face the harsh realities of what was also known as "separate development" another name for racial discrimination because it was not just separate but separate and definitely unequal. My white colleagues knew so little about people of color.

When I needed to use the toilet, I was told that there was a public toilet in the basement of the building for non-whites which I could use. I went there only once to find the toilet in a putrid condition; filthy and unkempt, with no toilet-paper or wash facilities. The first couple of days I struggled. I tried to drink very little, so that I would not need the restroom. Finally, I told my manager that it was not possible for me to use that toilet in the basement with broken doors, as it would pose a danger for me. He asked if I had any suggestions, or if I knew of any friends in the area who could help in this situation. I told him that I knew of a friend, Julie Govender who worked about three blocks away. Julie graciously allowed me to use the toilet at her workplace, as there were no whites in her office. At first, when I needed to use the bathroom, I would rush to the elevator, clamping my knees together, while hopping from foot to foot. I would run down Loveday Street to the building where my friend worked, ascend a flight of stairs to her office, and ... ahhhh ... relief! After a quick hello, I would run back, to continue my project in my corner of the office. As the weeks went by, I slowly gained confidence and left earlier for the restroom. Though I maintained a brisk pace, without the urgency of my initial days at work, I could actually take in the sights of the city; the cars and trucks on the busy street, the sweet aroma of fresh baked breads and pastries from the bakery. I would peek into the lavish department store windows to see what I may someday fancy.

On one occasion, I stopped quickly to try on a jacket that I had been eyeing through the window of a department store. As I entered, the sales associate immediately came to ask how she could help me. I asked if I could quickly try on the jacket, as I was on a short break. She made me wait while she helped the white ladies at the fitting room, that came out to ask if the garments they were fitting made their hips look too wide, or whether it fitted them well. As the white customers eyed me she said, "I'm so sorry, you're not allowed to try on the jacket, but I can try it on for you, so that you can see how it looks on me before you purchase it." "No thank you," I responded to her "lovely" offer. I left the store hurriedly, and rushed back to my work. I had not been exposed to the major department store etiquette regarding me, because before this I would never have dreamed of shopping in such "expensive" stores.

Interestingly, after a conference in Sweden, during a brief stopover in Rome in 2005, our oldest daughter Priscilla hastily shopped for presents to bring back to her younger sisters. She asked a store clerk if she could try on a skirt and received the same response. The sales associate offered to try on the skirt for Priscilla.

Back at my office job, the more I learned, the more my manager became dependent on me. The workload had increased tremendously and the company could not afford to have me go a few blocks away every time I needed to use the restroom. At an office meeting, which I was never invited to attend, this dilemma was raised and the white women refused to have me use their restroom.

There were two five-stalled restrooms on our floor for women, one close to our department and the other a little further, on the other side of the elevators. Because I had become indispensable to my manager, and he needed me to keep up with production, he had no choice but to assign the further five-stalled restroom exclusively to me. All the white women in the office would line up, especially after lunch, to use the closer five-stalled restroom. Just a few days after I was given my own bathroom, I was in one of my 5 stalls and I heard someone enter and open the faucet (tap). As I exited the stall, a white woman, who was washing her hands, looked up at me in the mirror with a surprised expression on her face. Her surprise quickly turned to disdain as she blurted out rudely, "Why are you using the white restroom!?" Struggling to contain the emotion welling up inside of me, I heard myself calmly respond, "You may not have received the memo, that this is now my restroom, and I would appreciate it if you would kindly leave." She slowly walked out of my bathroom still looking back at me in shock.

Everything was done in compliance with the law under the Separate Amenities Act, which clearly stipulated that non-whites were not allowed to use the same facilities, as that of whites.

A few months later, on my recommendation, my friend was hired. After the first few computers were sold, that I had worked on as well, there were rumors of a company wide party to celebrate. Then on one afternoon, we could smell the aroma of a delicious meal nearby. Soon everyone was in the board-room enjoying a sumptuous meal and drinks, while the two of us who were uninvited, were left at our desks to work. One co-worker felt awkward and asked if she could bring us some food. We graciously declined her offer. I was accustomed to not being invited to the fabulous company Christmas parties and other events, but those were less awkward for them, because it was usually off site. Later when I moved to a different department, one of the white ladies, Tita, genuinely became my friend. It was so funny how she would relate the events of the Christmas parties to me, so I could feel involved. With hysterical laughter, she would share the details, such as whose dress was too short, who flirted with who, and who embarrassed themselves dancing ridiculously while drunk.

I became more and more skilled in my duties, and about 2 years later, a young white woman was offered a position to work with me. I trained her, but she was having a really difficult time learning the job. On many occasions I would have to do my job and hers, so that we could keep up with the demand. I always waited earnestly at the end of the month to receive my hard earned check, and take home some goodies for my kids. They knew that they usually got treats when mommy received her check. This month the manager walked in and handed me my check. I opened it and was elated to find that I had received a huge bonus. The amount on the check was more than double the amount I usually earned. I ran into his office to thank him. While saying thank you I glanced back at the check, and realized that it was made out to the young white lady that I had been training. I then realized that he had mistakenly given me the wrong check. I was appalled. The manager sat me down and explained that whites were on a different pay scale in South Africa, and that they had to abide by the law of the land. He said that the system of Apartheid was to blame. With tears in my eyes, I handed the check back to him while he handed me my expected check. With a lump in my throat, and though in such desperate financial need, I had to uphold my human dignity. I emptied my desk and walked out with a sinking feeling of despair.

On that fateful day, as I left my desk, with a few belongings in a box, and walked to the elevator, I ran into Mr. Dalton, a manager of another department in the company, who was always very friendly and encouraging to me, though I never worked directly with him. When I told him that I had just resigned from my position, he was shocked and said that my manager had always spoken very highly of me. He asked if I would consider coming back to work for him for more pay, and soon after was hired by him. His reception area was very disorganized, so I got it in order in a few days. I took work home and alphabetized all of his files so he could easily find customer invoices, that were stacked out of order. He asked how I had organized the reception desk so rapidly. I told him that I had taken files home to work on at night. He insisted that I add the extra hours to my time sheet. Mr Dalton was one of the kindest men I worked with. When he heard that my 5 year old child, Ursula, was in the hospital and saw how worried I was, he would arrange for the delivery drivers to take me to see her during my lunchtime at Coronation Hospital, a Coloured/Indian hospital in the township of Newclare. He knew that the trip alone was more than twenty minutes each way, but insisted that they would be ok without me at the office while I spent the entire visiting hour with my little one at the hospital in the large children's ward, which housed about 50 children.

Black Money, White Money

At the end of the month, when I received my check, I would go directly to the bank to cash it. This was my first introduction to the South African banking system. Because whites were a minority in the country, their lines were usually short, with not many in it, but the line (queue) for non-whites was usually very long, simply because we were the majority.

At that time, not many blacks had bank accounts, but we all needed our checks cashed at the end of the month. We had to stand in a separate line that went out the door and sometimes around the building, to cash our checks.

One particular month, Tita asked if I wanted to accompany her to the bank. When we got there, I decided that this time I was going to stand in line with her. I knew that the whole room had their eyes on me, but I stood there pretending not to notice. Tita deposited her check and went to the door to wait for me. When I got to the teller, she told me that I was in the wrong line and had to go to the non-white line. Hiding my fear, I asked her firmly if black people and white people had different money and if it was placed separately and used differently at the bank. By this time some of the white people in line behind me were agreeing with me nodding their heads and giving their assent for me to stand with them. Visibly shocked and taken aback by my response to her, she just went ahead and processed my check for payment after looking at my identification. Fortunately, she did not call the police or I could have been arrested.

By the time I left that company we had five children. My fifth child was born while I was an employee. Sam and I started seriously discussing how we wished to leave South Africa, the country of our birth. We wanted to spare our children the humiliation that we had to face, on a daily basis.

I am thankful to God that the experiences, while at this company, despite being painful, opened my eyes further to the reality of life in South Africa. I knew without a doubt that these laws of Apartheid were man-made and not God inspired, like the government wanted us to believe. Now that I had children, I certainly did not want them to feel inferior like I did growing up, and thus tried to defy the laws against us, whenever I could, so they would know for a fact that they were all created equal in the eyes of God.

Back at the dinner table, as I concluded sharing my experience at my job, my six children looked at me in awe. Neil finally broke the silence: "Ok mom, you win, I'll share our bathroom at home with my five sisters."

Job Advertisements from South African newspapers in 1985 asking for "whites only" or "Europeans only," a term used in South Africa to refer to white South Africans.

21

THE 17TH SUITCASE

by Samuel Moonsamy

ONE Saturday morning as we were trying to declutter our garage for the umpteenth time in our home in the San Francisco Bay Area, at Oakland, I stumbled across this little brown bag, actually a little suitcase. As I dusted it off, my mind went back to the first time we used this little suitcase, on November 10th, 1985.

We had packed altogether sixteen bags, two for each of us with mostly personal effects, like clothing and some memorabilia, though not much. Because of the lack of space, Priscilla, our oldest, had offered candy to her younger siblings, in exchange for some of their suitcase space for some of her textbooks and sentimental possessions, with which she did not want to part.

After giving away the last of our possessions, by the time we left home, we were disoriented with excitement and perhaps some confusion. Never before had we all travelled together anywhere outside of Southern Africa as a family, let alone by airplane. Only Priscilla had accompanied her grandmother once on a short flight from Johannesburg to Durban. The rest of our kids had never been on an airplane before and the excitement mounted. Faster heartbeats coupled with inexorable sadness to leave our homeland, our family, our friends and even our dog, Tipsy, was beyond telling. As we said goodbye to our little pup, we fondly recalled adopting him from a neighbor whose dog had delivered a litter. Our kids had specifically chosen him because of his beautiful black shiny coat of fur. He was cute and clumsy as ever, and would tip over easily as a little pup, while running. Thus, his well chosen name.

On our way to the airport we made an important stop to bid farewell to my mom. She refused to come to the airport, knowing how difficult it would be, to say goodbye to her children and six grandchildren, whom she had helped raise. This was the most difficult, heart wrenching farewell.

Sick to the stomach, upon arrival at the airport, completely beyond our wits, we counted our bags again, checking labels provided by the travel agent. Counting sixteen suitcases, instead of carrying on the 17th, we asked if we could also check-in this unusually small brown imitation leather bag, 14" by 8" by 4", weighing less than a kilogram, about 2lbs, the entire little space inside filled with curry powders and spices. From our experience while visiting some parts of the United States, to arrange for our emigration, Sue and I believed that these spices were unobtainable there.

The South African Airways label on each suitcase, featured the motif of the flying Springbok with embossed white letters on a dark blue background in strictly two languages, English and Afrikaans. The label read SAL, Suid Afrikaanse Lugdiens and SAA, South African Airways. Next to the imprinted "Name" and below "Naam" was written apparently in Priscilla's neat handwriting: "Sam Moonsamy." Address (and Adres) again in both languages, The street number on 48th North Terrace Street, Kansas City, Kansas 66104. Telephone (Telefoon). The South African Airways label reminded me of the British and Dutch who had governed South Africa for several generations now. They had demanded that we learn the two official languages, English and Afrikaans. Every sign on every street, at the airport, and wherever we went in the country, had to be in both languages. Children were required and compelled to learn and pass both of these languages at school, to be promoted to the next grade. All of this, to honor and promote the political ideologies of the two majority European races, completely ignoring the multilingual people of South Africa and their most attractive languages, like Zulu, Sotho, Xhosa, Tamil, Hindi, and a kaleidoscope of other languages. The decision to entertain English and Afrikaans was merely to appease and satisfy these two colonial powers who had fought a war with each other and then made peace, with the understanding that their languages would dominate the South African scene, undermining all others as secondary, or of no value.

At the airport in Johannesburg, then named Jan Smuts, I hurriedly checked through the wad of dollar notes which we had exchanged from the South African currency, rands. I found that in the rush and flurry of airport buzz, I had been given a thousand dollars short by the bank teller. I rushed back again with a sinking feeling and blood rushing to my brain, to tell the teller that he had given me less money. He calmly counted and refunded the money without question. Knowing that because I had stepped away from the teller's desk, he had the right to deny my request, but for some reason unbeknownst to me, he had the money put aside and gave it to me without difficulty, yet without acknowledging fault. Usually white people in command, like bank clerks and others, were not obligated or accountable to people of color, but this man appeared to be in shock that I had returned and tendered me the money immediately. My last business transaction on South African soil, served as a stark reminder of what I was leaving behind. Black people dared not question white people, and white people, with their authority given to them by a flawed system, did not have to bow to requests of black people or face recrimination or censure for any wrongdoing.

Surrounding us at the airport were all of our family and many friends looking at us sadly, some crying. It was night as we said our final goodbyes. Tears streamed down our cheeks and flowed freely down the faces of beloved family and dear long-time friends. We looked back at every opportunity, as we moved toward the entry gate, knowing that this could be the last time we would see some of the familiar faces that had come to bid us farewell. With mixed feelings, we proceeded through the checkpoints each with our R999 (South African Rand) ticket in hand, allowed by the deposit on the sale of our home.

It is amazing how quickly while standing in line, carrying bags, and struggling to take care of tickets, passports, and other important details, the mind can divert from the pain of breaking loose from kith and kin. Then, as you settle into the confined quarters of your airline seat, you begin to realize that you are actually leaving your home, and all that you know. You may never come back, and you have the sinking feeling in the pit of your stomach as your wife and children look to you for courage in their nervous anticipation. The uncertainty of the unknown future grips your mind and you begin to sweat with fear.

The first leg of our journey took us to New York, The Big Apple, after a 17 hour trip with one stop to refuel at Isla de Sal, the Island of Salt, on the Cape Verde Islands off the coast of West Africa. Noelene our youngest asked me many times, "Daddy are we there yet?" Eager to get off after the first eight hour leg of the trip, we walked from this huge Boeing 747 that stood like a massive giant on a tiny island, warm and humid, to enter the simple transit lounge. Without knowing, we washed and brushed in cold salt water. The taste of salt lingered. Back on the plane, we asked for coffee or tea to break the sordid salty taste in our mouths. We later learned from other passengers that there were taps (faucets) for drinking water that we had somehow missed in the transit lounge. Had it been today, we would have purchased bottled water, which would have sounded ridiculous, to our South African ears, at that time.

Our plane took off again and eight hours later, at around 6am, we were flying over massive skyscrapers with a glimpse of the sun peering through the clouds. The excitement of seeing New York from the sky gave us an immeasurable feeling of joy. Finally, we were flying over the world famous city, viewing the buildings, cars and the skyline with the Statue of Liberty beckoning and ready to welcome and enfold us in the land of the brave and the free. The sounds going through our minds were like the final triumphant Hallelujah Chorus of the Messiah. We had arrived!

Standing in long lines, clearly indicating "foreign passports" we tended our files and were endorsed in with our passports signed, stamped and ready to go. Following crowds of people from everywhere we came to the arrival lobby area and saw this tall gentleman carrying a board clearly marked

"MOONSAMY FAMILY," the most welcoming sign I had ever beheld, in the hands of Pastor Robert Hayden. I had arranged for him to take us to a motel where we could rest for a couple of nights and then continue on to Kansas City, Kansas.

Carrying our bags with strong arms he helped to place them into the 15 seater church van. When we were all finally seated, he said, "Today is Veterans Day in the US, the 11th of November and since you plan to leave soon, I will give you a quick ride through the city and show you some of the well-known sights."

Our family, excited after a harrowing and tiresome 17 hour journey, was eager and ready to follow our newfound mentor and friend who expertly steered the big van through some narrow and some broad, but all busy streets. It was around 10 am, and even though a public holiday, there were crowds of people crossing the streets everywhere. The bustling traffic was unending, with yellow taxi cabs, people and cars passing by, some travelling alongside us on the right side of the road, which was the wrong side of the road to us. This amazing minister, already in his late seventies, caused us to gasp as he whisked through crowded lanes of traffic with ease. I later joked and told Pastor Hayden's congregation that more people prayed in his car than in his church.

We passed by the Empire State Building, Music City, the United Nations Building and several other places like the Twin Towers, and then headed back to First Baptist Church on Washington and Jackson Streets, in Hempstead, Long Island. Our heads were swirling. Jet lagged and half asleep, we stopped in front of the house in the yard of the church building. Instead of dropping us at a motel, even though we were hesitant to accept such a generous offer, Pastor Hayden insisted that we reside at the parsonage as it was not in use at the time. It was a fully furnished vacant home on the church property. I could not believe the generosity of Reverend Robert Hayden, whom I had called without knowing, after I inadvertently came across his name and number in the church directory of the American mission agency that had just employed me.

After an in-depth application process with the US Consulate office in Johannesburg and the long awaited receipt of a visa to work in the US, I called Reverend Hayden and asked if he could please meet us at J.F. Kennedy airport and help navigate us to a motel where we could spend a few nights en route to Kansas City. He agreed without hesitation to meet us. Being very careful not to scare him, I at first told Pastor Hayden that my wife and I would be coming. Then I added that we have six children and with much trepidation and hesitancy, I said "and, and, we have seventeen suitcases, one of them of course is very small with curry powders and other spices." "And what more do you have?" he inquired with a friendly voice, "... a couple of lions and elephants?" At this, we both broke out in loud laughter and I assured him that this was all, and that we were not bringing any wild animals with us. He immediately assured me that this would not be a problem to him as he had a big enough van to carry us all with our luggage. I hung up the phone with a sigh of relief and a heart filled with gratitude that God had begun to provide for us even before the commencement of this trip. "Thank you Lord, you are in control of our lives and you will, if necessary, make a way through the Red Sea, like you did for the children of Israel," I prayed.

The Big Apple

In welcoming us to this warm comfortable double story, three bedroomed duplex, Pastor Hayden also told us that we had this house to live in for as long as we needed. It belonged to the church, a parsonage for the pastor, but he and his wife had chosen to reside elsewhere.

Soon after, there were knocks on the door as families from the church delivered food such as pizza and chicken casserole, with warm welcoming smiles, looking at us with wonderment and curiosity, for not many had met people from Africa before. Some of them were under the impression that people from Africa did not speak English. Jokingly, I told them that we had traveled by "Jumbo" the elephant and later explained that I had meant a Jumbo Jet.

Our first night on a busy street was interrupted by loud police, ambulance sirens, and heavy traffic, yet we were still so excited about the prospect of being in a free country already enjoying the freedom which we also felt in the very air we were breathing.

Early the next morning Pastor Hayden appeared at our front door, with a box of fresh warm donuts. Later that week, our children accompanied Rev. Hayden to a burger place called Roy Rogers where they enjoyed mouth watering hamburgers and fries with unlimited sodas. With each new experience we were more and more excited during those first few days in the US.

Welcome to America

We called the Mission Agency that had employed us, and the voice on the receiving end of the call sounded shocked that we had indeed arrived. Apparently everybody thought it impossible for a large family with very little resources to board a plane ten thousand miles away and fly over the Atlantic to arrive in the biggest city in the world, New York City. "Yes, we have arrived" I assured them. "All eight of us with seventeen suitcases, including a little one filled with spices" such as the spices that early travelers, crisscrossed the globe to acquire from India.

The person on the phone hesitantly and haltingly said, "Welcome to America." Cautiously I replied, "Thank you. Now what next?" Apparently at a loss for words, the voice on the other side said, "We look forward to seeing you at the candidate school staff orientation, in January." Not wanting to sound ignorant about our whereabouts I asked, "Where?" and was curtly told "in Los Angeles, California. What's your plans?" the voice on the other side asked. My plans? I thought, I have none and am waiting to hear from you. After an awkward brief silence, she said, "Hope you get settled and we look forward to seeing you. God bless and goodbye."

Looking flustered and feeling deeply worried and concerned, I looked at Sue and said, "we're on our own, God be with us. Don't let the kids hear about this." In tears we clasped hands and bowed before God committing our lives, our children, and our future into His hands and into His care. Looking at us and the visible disappointment on our faces, Pastor Hayden later held hands with us and prayed for us. Despite the news of the day, we remained determined not to look back but to continue to look to the Lord who had promised "never to leave us, nor to forsake us."

Listening to our experiences first hand, it was difficult for Pastor Hayden to comprehend that the system of Apartheid, about which he had often read and heard, was far more serious than what he could have imagined. Together we spoke for hours about the deep seated fear of the ruling party in South Africa who felt that Apartheid had proudly offered the ultimate solution to the "race problem," also a vexing issue in America, we learned, and in many countries of the world.

A few days after our arrival in New York, on November 15th, we celebrated our youngest daughter's 11th birthday. All of us together sang "happy birthday" to Noelene at the Hayden's home in Hempstead, over a delicious chocolate cake baked by Mrs Hayden. We asked Rev. Hayden to pray for the birthday girl, a special dedication which we have carried out for all of our children, on their birthdays.

On Wednesday evening following our arrival, Rev. Robert Hayden scheduled Sue to speak at their church. The church was virtually full for a Wednesday Prayer Meeting and Sue was excited to share her story for the first time in another country. Everybody sat in rapt attention and when the meeting was over, Rev. Hayden announced that the people were now dismissed, but he said, "I am going to stay right here listening to the Moonsamy children sing." Almost the whole congregation decided to stay, and by the time the meeting finally ended and everybody dispersed into the dark, it was almost 11 pm and extremely cold outside. When we got out of the church, we moved as fast as we could to get to the house about 300 feet away, closing the door behind into the comfortably warm atmosphere of the house we were to occupy for the rest of the week.

Though tired, we were so overwhelmed that we stayed up late talking about the pastor and the people of the wonderful church family in New York, who seemed moved and highly appreciative of Sue's talk. We mused about some words that were not in common use, instead of stones, for example, people said "rocks" and for "biscuits" they say "cookies." Referring to people as "Coloured" was not acceptable, though in South Africa, a significant part of the people known by this designation are considered an independent racial entity. A Black American man said to me, "They decided to be nice to us and instead of calling us by the "N" word, decided to call us "Colored." He continued with a laugh, "Why particularly call us Colored, we are all Colored, some are colored white, some brown and some black; so you see brother, we are all Colored." Many people asked if the word "Afrikaner" referred to a black person in South Africa. We explained that the Afrikaner is of European origin, formerly Dutch and that the language of Afrikaans is derived from the Dutch language.

Another common observation we found was that people, even after we explained that we are from South Africa, would ask questions about India. One man asked if I knew his friend, Patel in Bombay, which is now named Mumbai. He broke out in laughter when I told him that there were about a hundred million Patels in India, and jokingly asked which one he was referring to. Again and again I patiently explained that at the time, I had never been to India but I was nationally African and ethnically Indian. Our grandparents were brought from India to South Africa by the British in 1860, as indentured laborers, to work in the sugarcane plantations. When people sometimes ask, "Why were you not born in India?" I jokingly reply, "because, I wanted to be near my mama." Someday I hoped to visit the land of my foreparents. We maintain some of our Indianness culturally and ethnically. Otherwise we are pukka South African.

For this reason, when I speak to groups of people, I often give a few expressive rhythmic lines as an introduction:

> *I have my ROOTS in India,*
> *I have my SHOOTS in Africa, and right now,*
> *I have my BOOTS in America.*

Kansas City, Kansas

Roughly a week after we reached New York, we departed with Braniff Airlines to Kansas City, Kansas on a $99 per person, one way flight.

A fellow South African pastoring in the United States at the time, Reverend Chris Martin, along with two couples, Jack and Clarice Hearon and James and Sharon Iverson, were waiting to meet us as we walked off the plane. Expecting that arrangements had been made for a rental, we learned that the house reserved for us was no longer available because the owners felt that we were too large a family to occupy this house. Rev. Martin arranged for us to live with the Hearons and the Iversons, while we searched for another rental. Though we tried our utmost to insist they not do so, Mr. and Mrs. Hearon gave up their beds for us. They drove us everywhere to shop for necessities, and to speak in churches where we were scheduled to speak. As much as they were fascinated with us, we too were completely fascinated by the Hearons for though American, they spoke with an accent that was fun to hear. They told us that they were from the South and wanted us to accompany them to Mississippi sometime. Hence their southern drawl which sounded so intriguing, though difficult for our South African ears to comprehend at times. We laughed, ate, and talked daily about the situation under Apartheid, a word very few Americans could pronounce. While trying to explain the term and give the correct pronunciation, I inadvertently told them, "you see it's like Apart-hate," as it occurred to me that the word pronounced like hate, did in fact originate from hate.

While in Kansas City, our children were fortunate to attend Muncie Christian School. This was their first experience attending an American school, where they had the freedom to express themselves and talk to the teachers. This was foreign to them, as in South Africa some teachers freely administered corporal punishment.

Our first Thanksgiving was something to behold. We, with our dear friends Rev and Mrs Brown and their two sons Marlin and Methven, who had also just relocated to Kansas from Eldorado Park South Africa, were graciously invited by the Woods family to our first ever Thanksgiving celebration. Never before had we seen such a huge turkey, and we all enjoyed the traditional sumptuous meal set before us. What tickled our children so much was that Americans ate pumpkin as a dessert in a pie. Marlin whispered to our kids how strange this was, as they quietly giggled. We were raised on pumpkin braised with onions, salt, and pepper as a side dish but never as a dessert. As the years went by, we developed a taste for pumpkin pie, and now cannot celebrate Thanksgiving without a delicious pumpkin pie topped with fresh whipped cream, sprinkled with a dash of nutmeg.

After spending about a week with the Hearons and the Iversons, we found a house and were getting ready to move on Sunday, the first of December in 1985 to a three bedroomed house near State Avenue with no furniture. The owner of the house had learned that we had no furniture and left a king-sized bed for us and also a lampstand. After church we ate lunch at McDonalds and Priscilla collected all the paper cups, plastic forks, knives, and spoons, to bring home as we had nothing, except the bed in the house. Fortunately there was central heating and also a stove that we could use to cook on.

We talked about how we were going to spend the night in this virtually empty house. We planned to turn up the heat and sleep on the king bed and the floors. We were just glad that we had a place that we could call home. At that time, there was a knock on the door and when we answered, we were surprised that three of the local pastors had a truckload of furniture to offload for us. They had heard of us and asked the members of their churches that morning, for donations of furniture and other items to establish a home. We later learned their names: Pastor James Gray of Oak Grove Baptist Church, Pastor Houchin, of Stony Point Baptist Church, and Pastor Daniel, J. Griffin, of Olivet Baptist Church. With helpers, they carried the furniture and boxes of linen, utensils and virtually everything we needed into our home. By nightfall, every room in this house was furnished. Three angels, pastors, came to our aid. Together we thanked God for His providential care and for these wonderful people who so graciously and sacrificially worked so hard to help us in our time of need.

We will always remember, that in the morning we moved into an empty house on December 1, 1985 and by nightfall the entire house was fully furnished. To God be the glory.

After just two months in the frigid cold of Kansas City, Kansas, I received a call from a warm, friendly minister, Reverend Gerald Duckett, of Grace Baptist Church in Yuba City, California. He wanted me to consider working with him as an associate pastor. While speaking with Rev Duckett, Sue whispered in my ear, "Ask him, if there's any snow in California?" Diplomatically, I asked, "How's the weather out there?" He intuitively answered, "Sunshine? There's plenty of sunshine in California, just like in South Africa."

Soon after, we found ourselves on a greyhound bus en route to California! We planned to fly, but our children asked if we could take the bus instead, so that we could see America. We obliged and embarked on a two day and two night trip via Greyhound bus to Yuba City, a distance of about 1700 miles. Not long into our trip, we realized that a flight would have been a lot less tiring and more convenient, and even similarly priced, because of discounted airline fares after the holidays.

As quickly as we received the furniture and household items though very grateful, we had to pass it on to others. This done, we bade farewell to our beloved friends in Kansas City.

The Hearons and a few others came to see us off at the bus station, and some sped behind us for quite a while waving and shouting farewell until the next bus stop. It was a tearful parting, as we set off, not realizing that the trip that we had just begun, would last for such a long time. When we look back we wonder how we could have made this arduous, lengthy, cumbersome trip over mountain passes covered with snow, with several rest stops at fast food restaurants. As we looked at the treacherous roads we thanked God that we did not have to drive, especially since we were used to driving on the left hand side of the road in South Africa and had not yet driven here in the US, let alone in snow. Finally weary and worn out, we arrived in Sacramento, the capital of California, where we transferred to a local bus to travel our last 45 miles to Marysville, California.

Lenasia Times, November 1985; Courtesy: Waheed Camroodeen

Appeal Democrat Newspaper article. Yuba City, Jan 11, 1986

Welcome to Yuba City

From Sacramento we passed miles of fruit trees and rice paddies, soaking in the beautiful countryside all the way on the 99 freeway until we arrived at Marysville on the first celebrated Martin Luther King Jr Holiday in California, Monday, January 20th, 1986.

At the Marysville bus depot, just across the bridge from Yuba City, the driver counted our bags and I signed for them. There were seventeen suitcases with the seemingly insignificant, small, but important one, filled with hot spices, all the way from South Africa. "Seventeen bags" the driver sighed. "And what's in this small one?" Jokingly I said that it carried extremely explosive curry powders, unaware that a few years later, this joke would have gotten us into a lot of trouble, especially if used while travelling. The driver seemed proud that all of the bags had arrived safely with not one missing. He said that in most cases with so many bags being transferred from one bus to another, some would get misplaced, sometimes never found. "This was a record of success," he said. We were happy to see our little brown suitcase safely among all the other suitcases.

Within seconds, a large crowd of people from Grace Baptist Church emerged from the back of the buildings shouting "welcome" with streamers, flowers and balloons. After many pictures and hugs everyone got into cars and drove us to our rental on B Street, next to the Methodist Church. The people of Grace Baptist Church, were extremely kind, gracious and friendly to us, helping us get settled and adjusted to our newly adopted country. We have made lasting friendships that we cherish from our first days in California.

Grandma Lu

It was here in Yuba City, that we met Lucille Cantrill who amongst others played a key role in helping us get settled. She fell in love with all six of our kids who respectfully called her Grandma Lu, though she insisted that they just call her Lu. We fell in love with her as well. She was a beautiful person both inside and out, always dressed to a tee with shades of rose and pink and matching accessories. She let our kids know that she was now their adopted grandma. She drove them all over the place to restaurants and to fun activities such as miniature golf. On our birthdays, she brought over professionally baked birthday cakes decorated with our names. She had won a bid at an auction for a birthday cake for all family members for a year and laughed that the donors did not know that she had just "adopted" a family of eight! However, they were happy to comply, seeing her excitement and enthusiasm.

The first time Grandma Lu drove our children to the Capital of California, Sacramento, she told them about the "one way" streets, where cars travel in many lanes, only in one direction. Not to dampen her enthusiasm, our kids never told her that they came from the largest city in South Africa, with highways and roads that were often crammed with traffic, similar to those found in the bigger cities in America.

On another occasion when she was taking them to the mall in Sacramento, they got to the escalators and she strictly warned them, "Be careful of these stairs ... they move!" With a group of curious onlookers, she demonstrated how to get on to and off from the escalator. She announced to the audience curiously gazing at our kids, that they were her adopted grandchildren who had just recently arrived from Africa. She loved them and cared for them and did not want them to get injured.

Our children never told Grandma Lu that they were familiar with escalators in South Africa, and that they had also been up and down them in other large cities in the United States as well, such as Kansas City and New York City. They just giggled, sparing grandma the awkwardness. According to South African culture, elders are highly respected. Our kids saw almost every part of Sutter County travelling with grandma, even to view the two massive rivers, the Oroville Dam about thirty miles away, and the famous Sutter Buttes, the smallest range of mountains in the world. Did I say world? Well, that's what we were told.

Later on, when our son Neil got his learner's permit, and was driving with Grandma Lu, she gave him some advice, "Neil," she said, "when you want to switch lanes, you turn on your signal and then you have the right of way, so you just head over to the next lane and everyone else needs to give way." She was also very protective of her newly added grandkids. We are very grateful to her biological kids and grandkids who were so gracious to share this vibrant, amazing woman with us. She thought that no young suitors were good enough for her grandkids, questioning thoroughly any friends who visited, even if they were just friends. This led to some interesting and funny stories, about which we always laughed with her.

It was a sad farewell attending and participating in her memorial service not too long ago. Her memory is etched in our minds and will forever live on in our hearts.

Peaches, Peaches And More Peaches

During our stay in Yuba City California where some of the worlds best peaches, plums, and nuts were grown, for miles all around us, new family friends such as Dale and Verlene

Grandma Lu and Priscilla, September 1998

Wilkerson, Darrel and Jane Smith and their families, would bring us bags of delicious fruit. Later, the Smith's son, Eric, lived with us while attending school. We love Eric and our kids still call him their "brother from another mother." If we were not home, these church members would just leave these bags of fruit on our doorstep. One particular summer we were inundated with peaches. To add to our fortune, after speaking at a church in Newcastle, the pastor who was very appreciative that we had taken the time to speak and sing at his church, asked for my van (combi) keys and when we got in to leave, we found that they had placed about five bags of peaches in the van. We were too shy to tell them we were overloaded with peaches, so I told Sue not to worry as I was going to share them with some friends. When we got home, I loaded several bags in the trunk (boot) of the Ford and headed to our friends from India living nearby: "Hello Mrs. Ghinda," I said, "Would you like some peaches?" Not understanding much English,

Mrs. Ghinda repeated "Peachees, peachees!" and I nodded yes. With that she called her two little sons, talking to them in Punjabi. They hurried inside the house and came out with two huge bags of peaches! I tried telling her that I did not need any peaches, but she would hear nothing. Luckily she opened the back door instead of asking me to open the trunk, and placed them on the back seat. I drove back in stitches, convulsing with laughter at myself, because now we had even more peaches than what we could handle, peaches galore!

Fortunately, as always, to the rescue, came Grandma Lu. She saved the day for us by helping us to cut and peel loads of peaches, sprinkling some "Fruit Fresh" on them and stacking them in suitably sized plastic bags in the freezer; happily ever after we had enough for the winter months.

"If you abide in me and I in you, you shall bear much fruit." John 15:5

1970 Ford

The story of this big green vehicle is interesting, as I had never before driven a vehicle of this size and make. On our first evening in Yuba City, I got behind the wheel and quickly drove through the gateway of a church's parking lot, right next door. I drove around and around to accustom myself to this big vehicle with so much power. We had very few problems with this car though Pastor Duckett had told us what he believed an old F-O-R-D meant, "Fix Or Repair Daily." With this car I had to learn a whole new terminology related to automobiles like "gas" for petrol, "hood" for the bonnet, "trunk" for the boot, "glove compartment" for the cubby, "bodywork" for panel beating, "muffler" for silencer, "lug wrench" for wheel spanner, "turn signal" for indicator, but most important of all, I had to learn to drive on the right hand side of the road. Oh yes the road is known as the "pavement" in the US. In South Africa the pavement is what is called the sidewalk in the US. Thus, if drivers drove on the pavement in South Africa, it would be most dangerous. Fortunately, during our time in Yuba City, gas was about 70 cents a gallon (3.79 liters in the US) and I was able to fill up for about ten dollars, and travel with ease from one city in California to another, wherever churches invited us to minister.

On one occasion, while traveling back from a Saturday morning Prayer Breakfast at a town called Newcastle about 30 miles from Yuba City across the Interstate Highway 80, our car was negotiating a steep hill when it suddenly came to a halting stop preceded by several erratic shaking moves.

Looking back through my mirror, a string of cars were following and stopped behind us. I slowly rolled backward as none of them could pass this narrow and dangerous section. When I found an open spot, I moved until I was safely off the road. I then started walking to find a telephone booth, looking back to see if my family was still safe. On my return, I saw a little truck parked off the road near us. A tall, muscular, tattooed man wearing a tee shirt with ripped off sleeves, was talking to Sue. As I got closer, I heard him ask, "Do you have AAA? Do you have any money?" She replied "No." He then got back into his truck and left to return a few minutes later with a tow truck from an auto repair shop nearby. Unlike at the gas station in Machadodorp in South Africa, we received help from the tow truck driver this time. They towed my car to the repair shop, where he instructed the mechanic to repair the broken timing belt. At lunchtime he came back and asked me to accompany him to a restaurant nearby. Sue and the kids decided to grab a sandwich and shop at a store close by, to pass the time. I tried to order a burger and pay for our meals, but he insisted on buying the two of us each a steak entree. After a hearty lunch and in-depth conversation, he left again and returned in the evening with money to pay for the repair. I refused and took out my credit card but he insisted, just like Dominee Theron in South Africa. The two of us sat talking in the car afterwards when he looked me in the eye and asked, "Do you think that I am a good man?" I nodded my head affirmingly and responded, "yes, most certainly." He said, "Sam, I'm not a good man. I gave my dad a lot of grief and landed myself in a lot of trouble. You remind me of my father. He was a preacher like you. He travelled in an old broken down car like you. He never had any money, and never owned a AAA card, like you. "Today," he said, "when I saw your car on the side of the road, I heard someone say "turn back and help those people." I turned to my wife and said, "did you say something?" She said that she had not said a word. "I distinctly heard a voice again say "turn back and help those people." "I don't normally stop for people on the road, but immediately I swung my car around and came back to see what I could do to help." He broke down in tears and said "I have turned away from God and the beliefs that my father taught me as a child. I know God was speaking to me today." I asked if I could pray for him after telling him of God's amazing heart of forgiveness. He hugged me and thanked me for the prayer and then left.

By this time the pastor of the church had sent some people to take Sue and the girls to their home and also graciously offered to pay for the repair as he felt that we had driven to speak in their church that morning, but Lloyd insisted on paying. The next time we visited this church to speak, Lloyd and his wife Janet were there in the church to welcome us and to listen to us sing and speak.

Not very long after, at the candidate school for new staff, we met Dr Levert, president of a Bible College in Los Angeles. He introduced us to Dr Vernon McGee, known for his daily radio broadcasts of "Thru the Bible" and to Reverend and Mrs Moore. We immediately started a long and lasting relationship with the Moores, who became our children's second set of adopted grandparents in the US.

We often travelled with the Moore's and our trips with them were always fun filled. At one restaurant where I was competing to pay the bill, Rev Moore struggled with me for the opportunity to pay when I told the cashier, "Don't take his money. He's a foreigner and you can't trust his card." Upon hearing this, she quickly took my card instead.

In his Southern accent, he told me one time, "crack the window a bit." 'What in the world!" I said, "Are you suggesting that I break the window?" We teased each other over and over again. I loved his accent and tried imitating him, making him and his wife laugh a lot. Whenever we talked about South Africa, she used to say, "if I catch that Botha (she pronounced Bowta)," the South African president at the time, "I'll stomp on his toes." Grandma Moore did not like to fly so her husband, Carl Moore, drove her long distances. This gave her added room on the back seat and trunk, for her neatly boxed church hats as well. Grandma Moore passed away a few years ago and we miss her dearly but know that we will be reunited with her in heaven. Rev Moore at 93 years of age, still travels between Oklahoma and Sacramento driving for days at times, at least two or three times a year.

Rev and Mrs Moore with 4 of the Moonsamy adopted grandchildren

The Flood of 1986

After the orientation program in Los Angeles, we returned to find that Yuba City and the surrounding areas were threatened with rising rivers from the heavy rainfall and melting snow. The Oroville Dam nearby, was fast reaching its limit, ready to break loose. Neil and I walked across the bridge and looked at the swirling waters below, almost touching the bridge. Unknowingly we admired a dangerous situation, ignorant of the impending flood. Every day the television focused on Yuba City, warning that the levee (a word we had never heard before, referring to the riverbanks) was at saturation point and that water would soon be spilling its banks, immersing the city.

We were not aware how critical the situation was until Bill Webster, a CHP officer who also was a deacon of the church, and his wife Marilyn, told us to pack up and come over to their home as it was at a safer elevation. Nothing happened that night, but while Neil and I were shopping late the next afternoon, we suddenly heard sirens and rushed with everyone out of the door.

News reports confirmed that a levee had broken on the opposite side of the Feather River on February 20th, 1986, and that the city of Linda, directly affected was frantically moving out all the people and animals. The next morning we travelled on the highway above the town of Linda and saw buildings, including the mall, covered with water. Some people even went "deep sea" diving with snorkeling equipment to rob jewelry and other stores. I cannot say with certainty, but I heard that the police made some underwater arrests.

Our family called from South Africa because they had seen the floods on TV. They were gravely concerned and asked us to please come back to South Africa. When my mom called from Lenasia she wanted to talk with every child individually, to make sure that they were alive and well. I joked with my family telling them not to worry, that I was safe on the rooftop holding our wired phone.

The floods were beginning to subside. We could see the top of the red roof of a pizza place emerge, and several other buildings, including the mall. The damage and destruction was severe. We were none the worse for the experience, for never before have we been in a flood situation. The levee on our side of the river did not break. We prayed for the many who had lost their homes. The aftermath of natural disasters, such as hurricanes and heavy drenching rain, can cause havoc. I don't think you can get used to this, but Americans with amazing resilience just start all over again, building and rebuilding.

Move To The Bay Of San Francisco

In the late 1980's, images on the evening news of "Shanty Towns" erected by students at UC Berkeley to encourage divestment from Apartheid South Africa, caught the attention of our family. Two of our six children, Priscilla and Melanie, were accepted to UC Berkeley. As we helped our girls prepare for this new opportunity, we met the Jacobsons, and Pastor and Mrs Ferguson, who befriended us and extended an amazing helping hand to get them settled in the Bay Area.

When we visited our children in the San Francisco Bay Area we were pleasantly surprised to see such a beautiful rainbow of people from all parts of the world. We met people from other parts of Africa that we would never have had the opportunity to meet in South Africa, including Maurice from Ghana, an incredible young man whom we adore. He became a son to us and still addresses us as mom and dad. The weather in the bay was much like our mild South African climate. We soon fell in love with the beauty of the bay, especially the kaleidoscope of people. It felt like a little taste of heaven.

We decided to move the remainder of the family to the San Francisco Bay Area in the summer of 1988. Tearfully, and with heavy hearts, we bid farewell to our amazing Grace Baptist church family and wonderful friends in and around Yuba City, such as Dr and Mrs. Campbell, the Rice family, and so many more. After settling down in the bay area, we realized that we no longer needed to move, as the ground beneath us, moved on its own! In 1989 we experienced the Loma Prieta Earthquake. Thankfully we were all safe and prayed fervently for those who had lost so much during that time.

While in the bay area, we had the opportunity to meet Pieter-Dirk Uys, who was a well-loved, very popular, Caucasian

South African actor/comedian. He satirized the political situation in South Africa, to expose its absurdity, and strangely he was enjoyed by all, even many white people. He brought to light truth that was censored usually at the time, because he found a way to use humor to get his message across. He was funny and knew how to keep people laughing. For his shows, he dressed as a woman in order to impersonate some of the characters he played, the main one being Evita Bezuidenhout, an Afrikaner woman. I remember so clearly that as Sue walked to greet him on the deck of a home in Oakland, CA, her heel got caught in the opening of the wooden deck. She maneuvered it out and then reached forward to shake his hand remarking "Oh these heels are such a nuisance." He laughed and said, "tell me about it. I know exactly how you feel."

Though we like to focus on our positive experiences in cities across the United States, we know that God would want us to share some of our struggle as well. In one city in the USA, young people passing our house shouted from their cars several times, "Hindu, go home!" I mentioned this incident to the people at the church and horrified they asked, "so what did you do?" I replied, "I simply took their advice and went home, turned on the television, and made myself comfortable." Another phrase from me that elicits laughter at all times is when I tell people younger than thirty, "welcome to my country," a rather brave but funny thing to say, because I definitely arrived here before they did.

Sadly, our children have faced some of the same experiences. While in high school, when Neil tried to sit down on the school bus, kids covered the empty seats with their legs so he and other Indian kids would not be able to sit. Thus, he decided to bike to school. After school, students leaving in cars would yell racial slurs at him on his bike. On one occasion, someone hurled soda at him. On another occasion, a girl yelled something racist at him. Upset, he turned his head to look at her, and as soon as he turned his head back, he rammed into a stationary vehicle, knocking his front tooth out.

He wrapped the tooth in his shirt and wet it with water from someone's sprinkler. He got home with blood on his face and clothes, and we rushed him to our dentist in Grass Valley. Dr. Takeoka reinserted the tooth with the hope that it would take root again, but several months later it discolored and had to be replaced with a bridge. Interestingly enough, this experience allowed us to become even closer to the Takeokas, who became family to us. So many years later, Sue and I still travel all the way to Grass Valley from the Bay area to see them.

Though difficult, these experiences have made us stronger. We often face them with humor as well. I joke that I named our son Neil, after Neil Armstrong (one of the first astronauts to set foot on the moon), because our Neil was the first male child to set foot in the "Moon"samy home!

Though it may seem dismal at times, I know that by the grace of God, people's hearts can change and love and forgiveness can prevail. I hope that these stories will inspire people to see others regardless of color through the eyes of Jesus, who, *"when He saw the multitudes, His heart was moved with compassion."* Matthew 9:6. Though so polarized in our current political climate, we believe that people can work to break the barriers that tear us apart and find common ground where we can live together harmoniously.

God has graciously continued to pour His blessings on us in recent years. Our family has had the honor of being associated with ministries led by incredible servants of God such as the Cains, Howards, Huddlestons, Jacksons, Madsens, Martins, Metters, Rogers and Wrights, among many others, for which we are sincerely grateful.

Our family has more than doubled from eight to seventeen, with the addition of three sons in law, a daughter in law, and five grandchildren.

Our children are grateful for the opportunities they have had in the US, and in turn are giving back to their communities. Five of our children graduated from UC Berkeley, and one from Cal State, Hayward. Priscilla and her husband Alan, both scientists, have two kids; Kaitlyn, our soccer star, and Karissa, our dancer. Susheela, our second, a counselor, works at a high school in Oakland. Ursula, an optometrist, and her brother Neil, own a busy optometry practice in Oakland. Ursula and her husband Mario, also an optometrist, have a precious little six year old boy, Daniel. Melanie works as an academic advisor for student athletes at UC Berkeley. Her husband Wayne teaches at an elementary school in Oakland. Their children Alec excels in theatre, and Alisha in art. Neil's wife Patricia is a computer scientist working in IT. Our youngest child, Noelene, is an assistant professor of a family nurse practitioner program while also pursuing her doctorate in nursing.

Our six children still sing together and minister to people, as they did when they were little. They often sing a song by the group "Anointed," which includes these appropriate lyrics:

Every good thing I have done,
everything that I've become,
everything that's turned out right,
is because You're in my life,
and if I ever teach a child the way,
ever learn myself to change,
ever become who I want to be,
it's not the "I" but the "You" in me.

We are thankful to God for the wonderful journey of faith, for the many miracles, and for whatever the future may hold. We arrived in the United States over thirty years ago with six children and seventeen suitcases, including the little brown suitcase, probably intended for use by a small child, properly manufactured as a small suitcase, worn out and slightly bent but not dilapidated. This little brown suitcase has moved with us through many cities in America.

If this little suitcase could talk it would tell you how this journey began, where it led, and how we finally settled in Northern California. Though it cannot talk, it still conjures vivid and lasting memories to be told to the generations that will follow in this strong, faith based legacy.

THE END

The current family of 17

Sam and Sue with their grandchildren

The 17th suitcase

Photos archived by Neil Moonsamy.
Typeset in LaTeX by Patricia Derler.
Cover design by Patricia Derler and Melanie Moonsamy.
Book title by Kaitlyn Blair.

The Moonsamy Family is available for speaking and/or singing
engagements. Contact: moonsamyfamily1@gmail.com